Wandering through the Mugdock woodlands (Stage 1)

THE WEST HIGHLAND WAY

The first long-distance route to be officially designated in Scotland, the West Highland Way (Slighe na Gàidhealtachd an Iar) traces 96¾ miles (156km) from Milngavie on the outskirts of Glasgow to Fort William. The trail typically takes six to nine days to walk and is suitable for fit, healthy and experienced walkers.

Contents and using this guide

This booklet of Ordnance Survey 1:25,000 Explorer® maps has been designed for convenient use on the trail and includes:

- a key to map pages (pages 2–3) showing where to find the maps for each stage
- the full and up-to-date line of the National Trail
- an extract from the OS Explorer map legend (pages 52–54)

The companion guidebook – *The West Highland Way* – describes the full route from south to north (the 'classic' direction). It also includes lots of practical and historical information.

Cicerone's EU representative for GPSR compliance is Easy Access System Europe, Mustamäe tee 50, 10621 Tallinn, Estonia. Email gpsr.requests@easproject.com.

Second edition 2024
ISBN: 978 1 78631 178 8
Reprinted 2025
First edition 2016

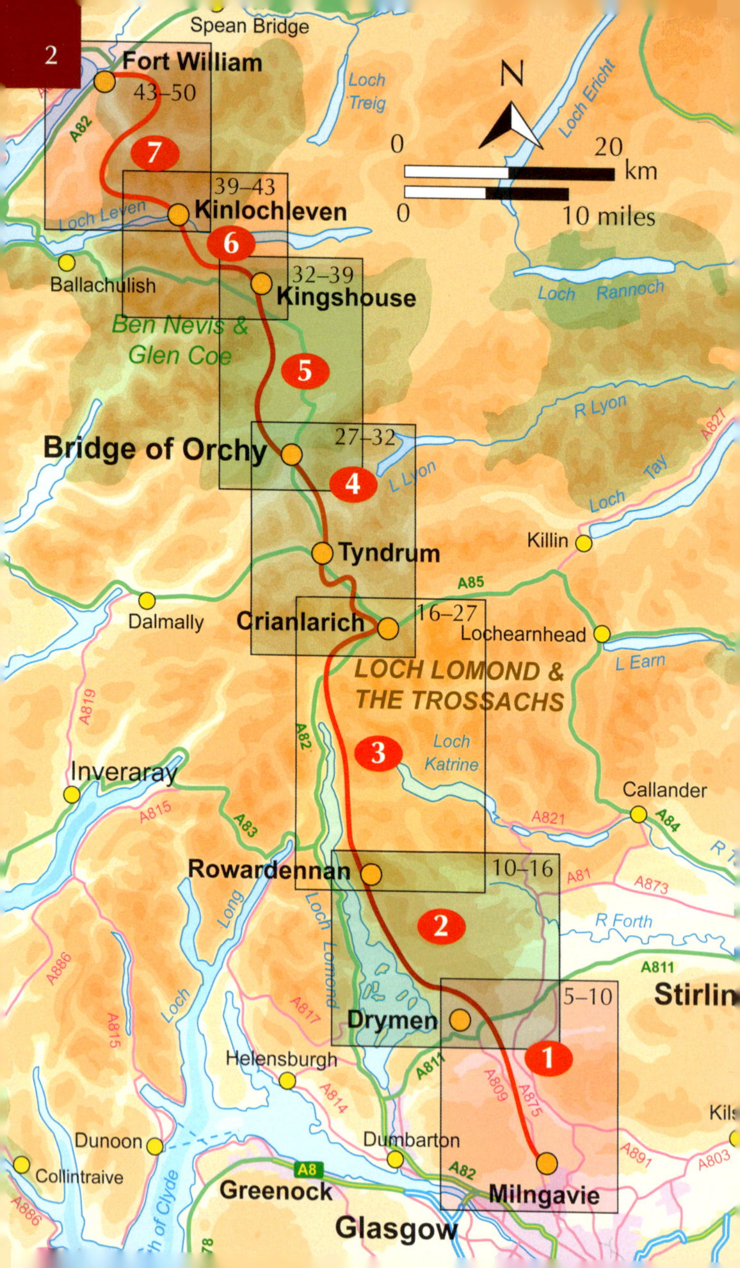
Spean Bridge
Fort William
43–50
A82
7
Loch Treig
N
0
20
km
0
10 miles
Loch Ericht
39–43
Kinlochleven
Loch Leven
6
Ballachulish
32–39
Kingshouse
Loch Rannoch
Ben Nevis & Glen Coe
5
R Lyon
A827
Bridge of Orchy
27–32
4
L Lyon
Loch Tay
Killin
Tyndrum
A85
Dalmally
Crianlarich
16–27
Lochearnhead
L Earn
LOCH LOMOND & THE TROSSACHS
A819
A82
3
Loch Katrine
Inveraray
A815
A83
Callander
A821
A84
Rowardennan
10–16
A81
A873
Long
Loch Lomond
2
R Forth
A886
A811
Stirlin
Loch
A815
A817
5–10
Drymen
1
Helensburgh
A811
A809
A875
A814
Dunoon
Dumbarton
A891
A803
Collintraive
A8
A82
Greenock
Milngavie
A886
Glasgow

THE WEST HIGHLAND WAY

Route symbols on OS map extracts

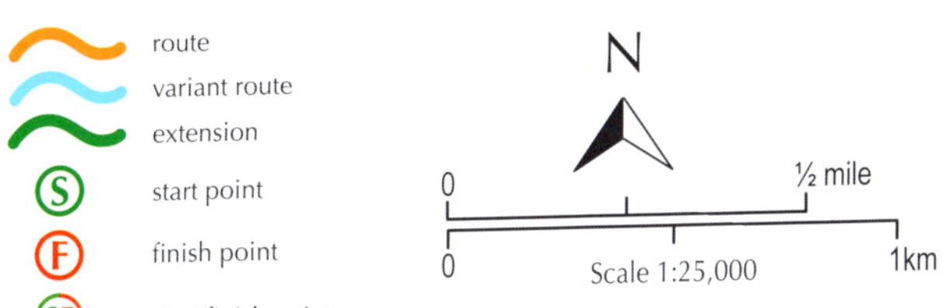

For OS legend see pages 52–54

Loch Ardinning
Jetty
Mugdock
Easterton Stables
Easterton of Mugdock
Middleton Farm
Middleton of Mugdock
Craigash
Water Treatment Works
Barrachan
Quarry (dis)
Mugdock Reservoir
Fords
Air Shaft
Air Shafts
Mugdock Loch
Tower
Mugdock Country Park
Moot Hill
Chapel (remains of)
Mugdock Castle (remains of)
Garden Centre
Gallow Hill
Craigend Castle
Gun Site (disused)
Mugdock Wood
West Highland Way
Waterfall
Allander
Craigallian
Kyber Cottage
Craigallian Bridge
Allander Water
Milngavie Golf Club
Laighpark
Boat House
Scroggy Hill
Lower Craigallian
Mount Zion
Works
Field Wood
Braval House
Low Craigton
Craigton Village

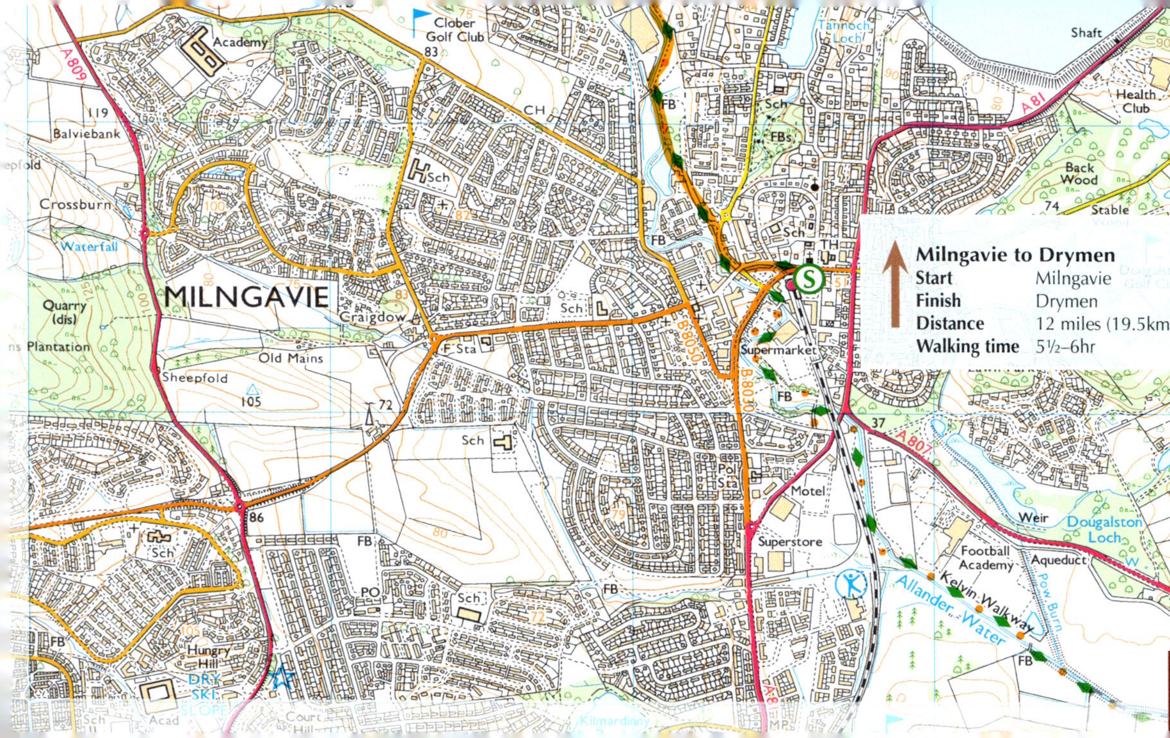
Milngavie to Drymen
Start Milngavie
Finish Drymen
Distance 12 miles (19.5km)
Walking time 5½–6hr
MILNGAVIE
Academy
Clober Golf Club
A809
Balviebank
Crossburn
Waterfall
Quarry (dis)
Plantation
Sheepfold
Old Mains
Craigdow
F Sta
Sch
CH
FB
FBs
TH
Tannoch Loch
Shaft
A81
Health Club
Back Wood
Stable
B8050
B8030
Supermarket
Pol Sta
Motel
Superstore
A807
Weir
Dougalston Loch
Aqueduct
Pow Burn
Football Academy
Kelvin Walkway
Allander Water
Beech Wood
Hungry Hill
DRY SKI SLOPE
PO
Kilmardinny

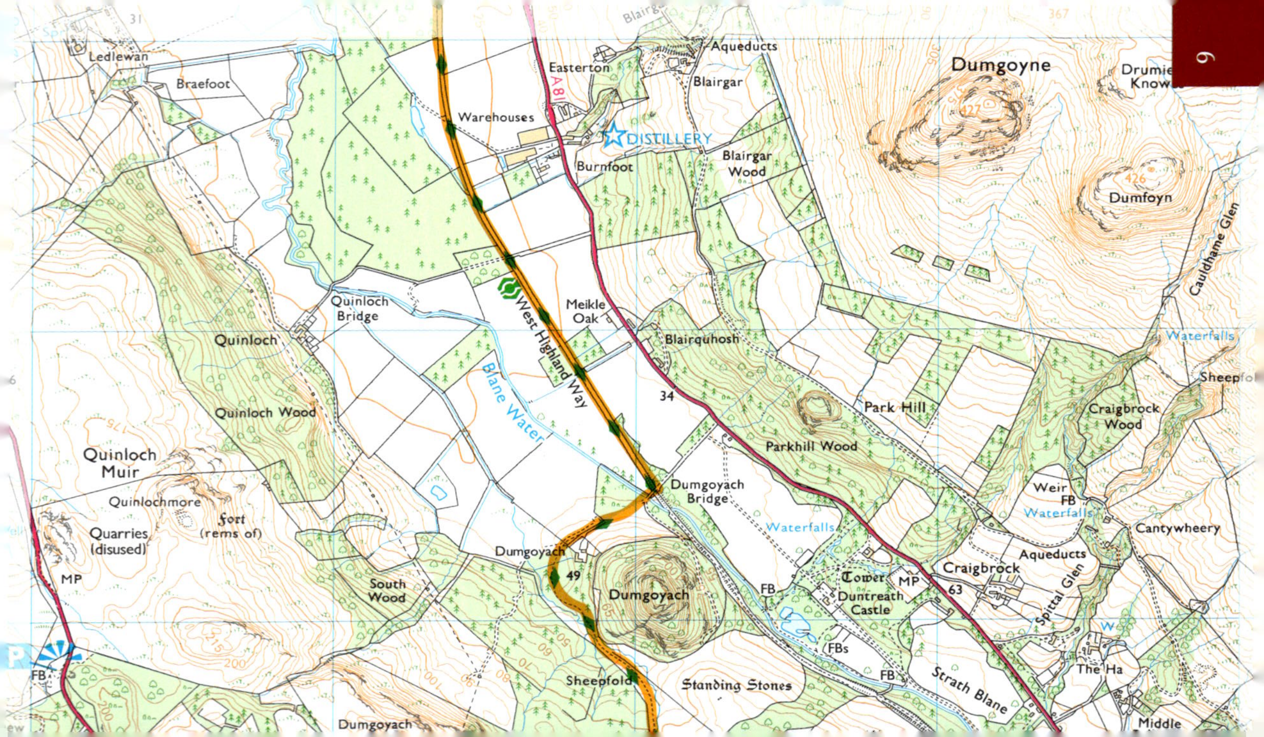
Dumgoyne
Drumie Know
Dumfoyn
Cauldhame Glen
Aqueducts
Easterton
Blairgar
A81
Warehouses
DISTILLERY
Burnfoot
Blairgar Wood
Ledlewan
Braefoot
Quinloch Bridge
Meikle Oak
Blairquhosh
West Highland Way
Quinloch
Quinloch Wood
Blane Water
34
Park Hill
Parkhill Wood
Craigbrock Wood
Sheepfo
Waterfalls
Quinloch Muir
Quinlochmore
Fort (rems of)
Quarries (disused)
MP
Dumgoyach Bridge
Waterfalls
Weir
FB
Waterfalls
Cantywheery
Aqueducts
Craigbrock
63
Spittal Glen
Tower
MP
Duntreath Castle
FB
Dumgoyach
49
Dumgoyach
South Wood
FBs
FB
Strath Blane
The Ha
Sheepfold
Standing Stones
Dumgoyach
Middle
FB

John Muir Way
West Highland Way
B 821
A 809
Cuilt
Cuilt Brae
Boards
Braehead
Blair's Hill
Alreoch
East Arlehaven
South Brae
Ardoch
Sewage Wks
Carbeth Loch
Easter Carbeth
Carbeth
Carbeth Hill
Carbeth Wood
Craigallian Loch
Loch Wood
Carglas Plantation
Dumbrock Loch
Craigmore
Garvel Bridge
Auldmurroch Farm
Lecher Burn
Auchineden Farm
Kilmannan Farm
Low Auchengillan
Townhead of Auchengillan
Craigmore Cottage
Outdoor Centre

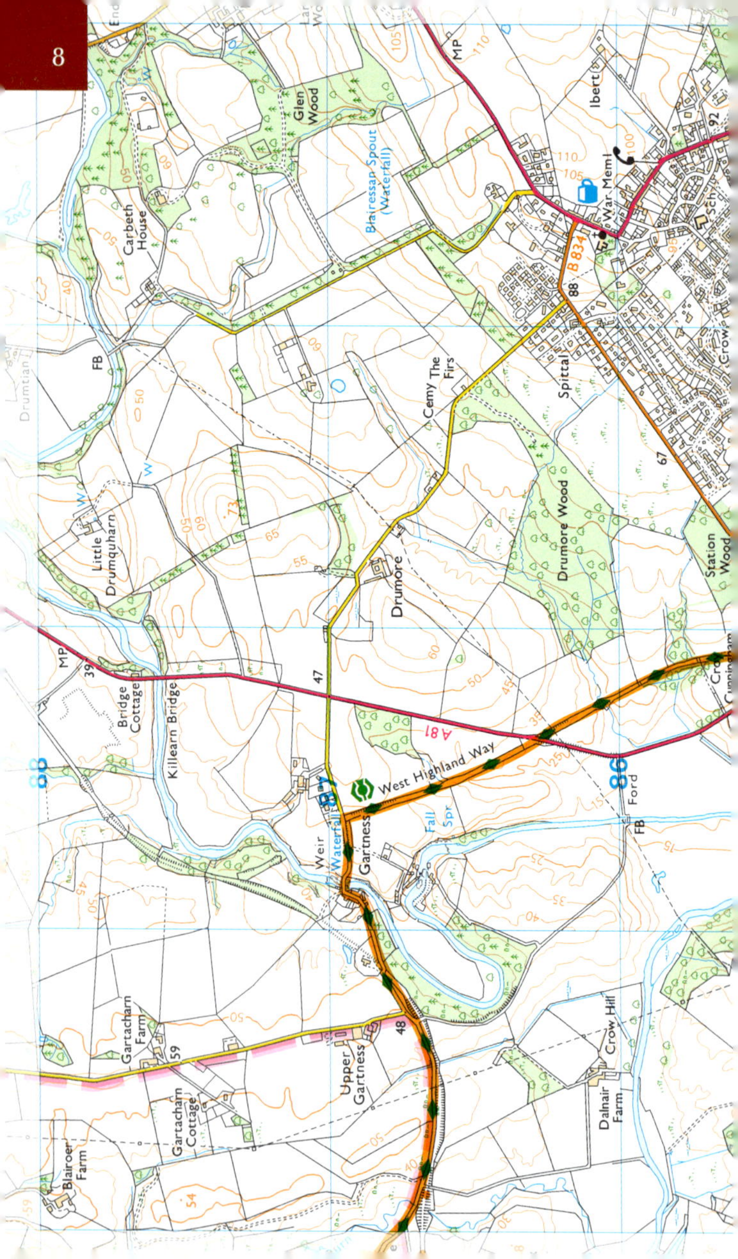
Glen Wood
Blairessan Spout (Waterfall)
Carbeth House
Ibert
War Meml
Sch
B 834
Spittal
Cemy
The Firs
Drumore Wood
Station Wood
Drumore
Little Drumquharn
FB
Drumtian
MP
Bridge Cottage
Killearn Bridge
A 81
West Highland Way
Weir
Waterfall
Gartness
Fall
Spr
Ford
FB
Crow Hill
Dalnair Farm
Upper Gartness
Gartacharn Farm
Gartacharn Cottage
Blairoer Farm

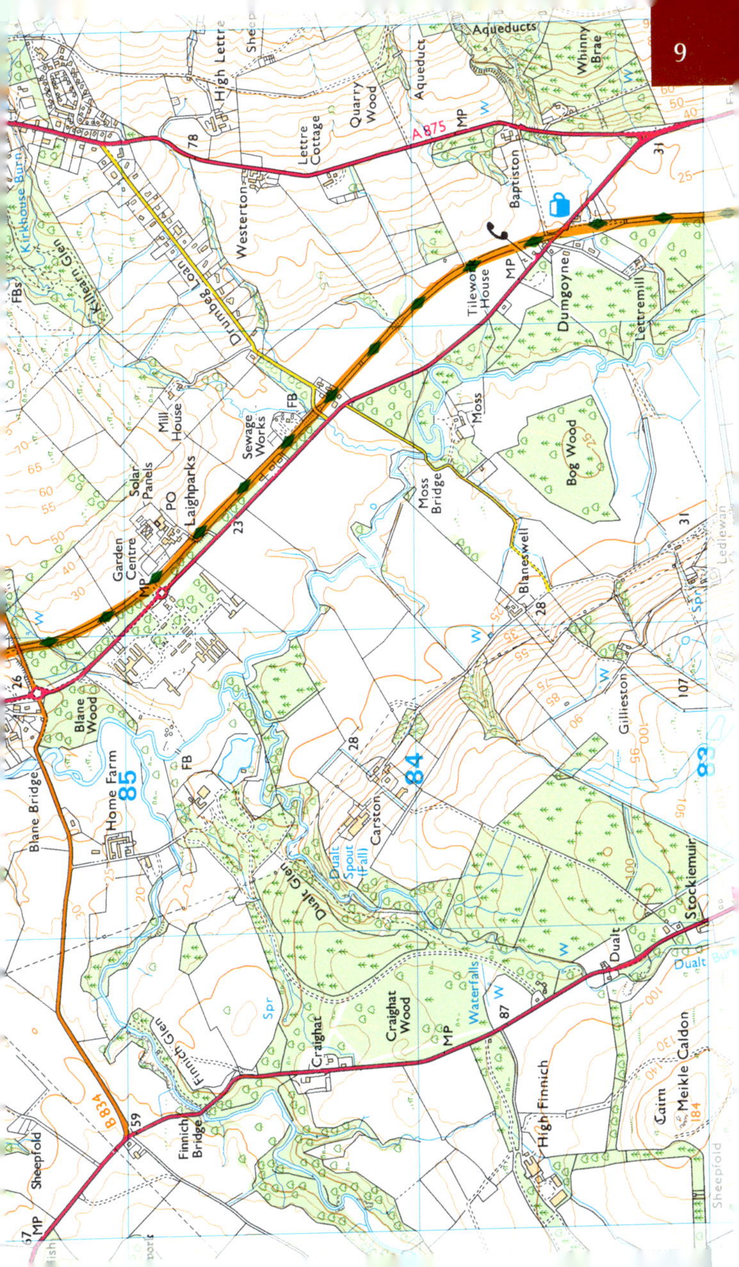
Aqueducts
Whinny Brae
Aqueduct
High Lettre
Sheep
Quarry Wood
Lettre Cottage
A875
MP
78
Westerton
Baptiston
31
Kirkhouse Burn
Killearn Glen
FBs
Drumbeg Loan
Tilework House
MP
Dumgoyne
Lettremill
FB
Mill House
Sewage Works
Moss
Bog Wood
Solar Panels
PO
Laighparks
Moss Bridge
Garden Centre
MP
23
Blaneswell
28
Ledlewan
Spr
26
Blane Wood
W
Gillieston
107
Blane Bridge
Home Farm
85
FB
28
84
Carston
83
Dualt Spout (Fall)
Dualt Glen
Stockiemuir
Dualt
Dualt Burn
Finnich Glen
Spr
Craighat
Craighat Wood
MP
Waterfalls
87
B834
59
Finnich Bridge
High Finnich
Meikle Caldon
Cairn
184
Sheepfold
MP
67

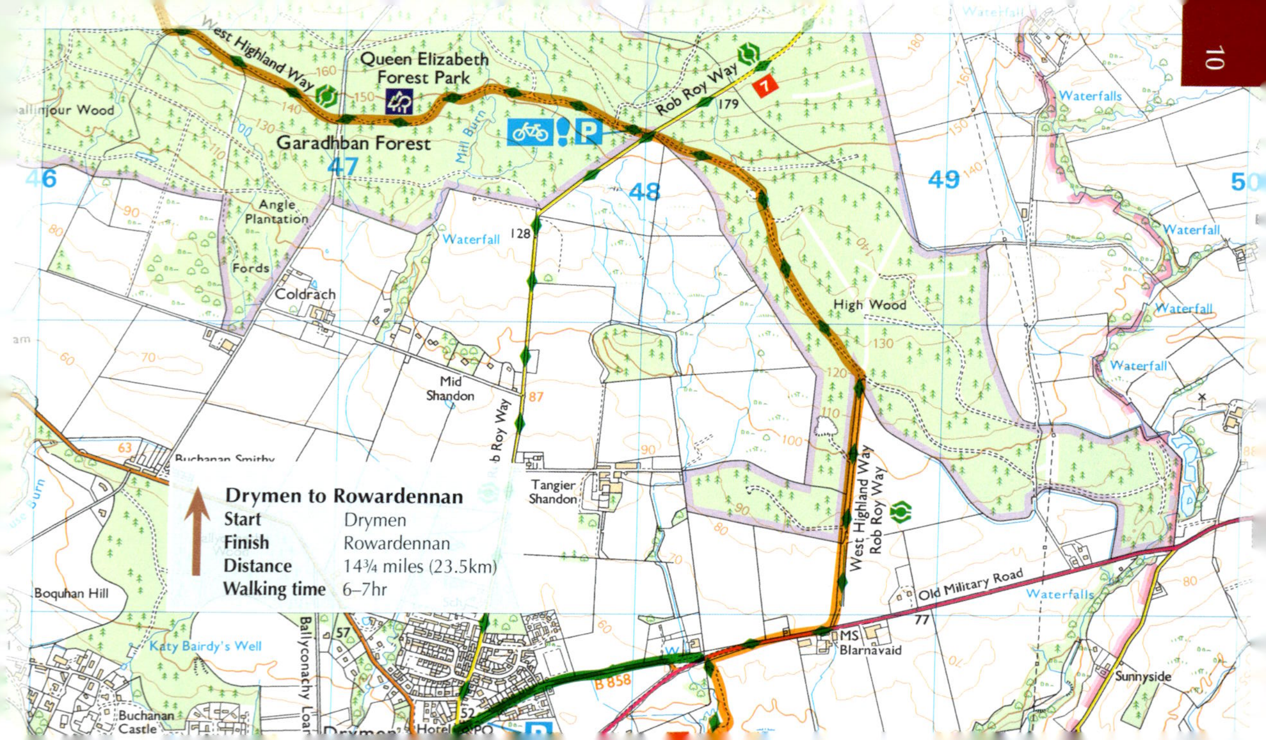

Drymen to Rowardennan

Start Drymen
Finish Rowardennan
Distance 14¾ miles (23.5km)
Walking time 6–7hr

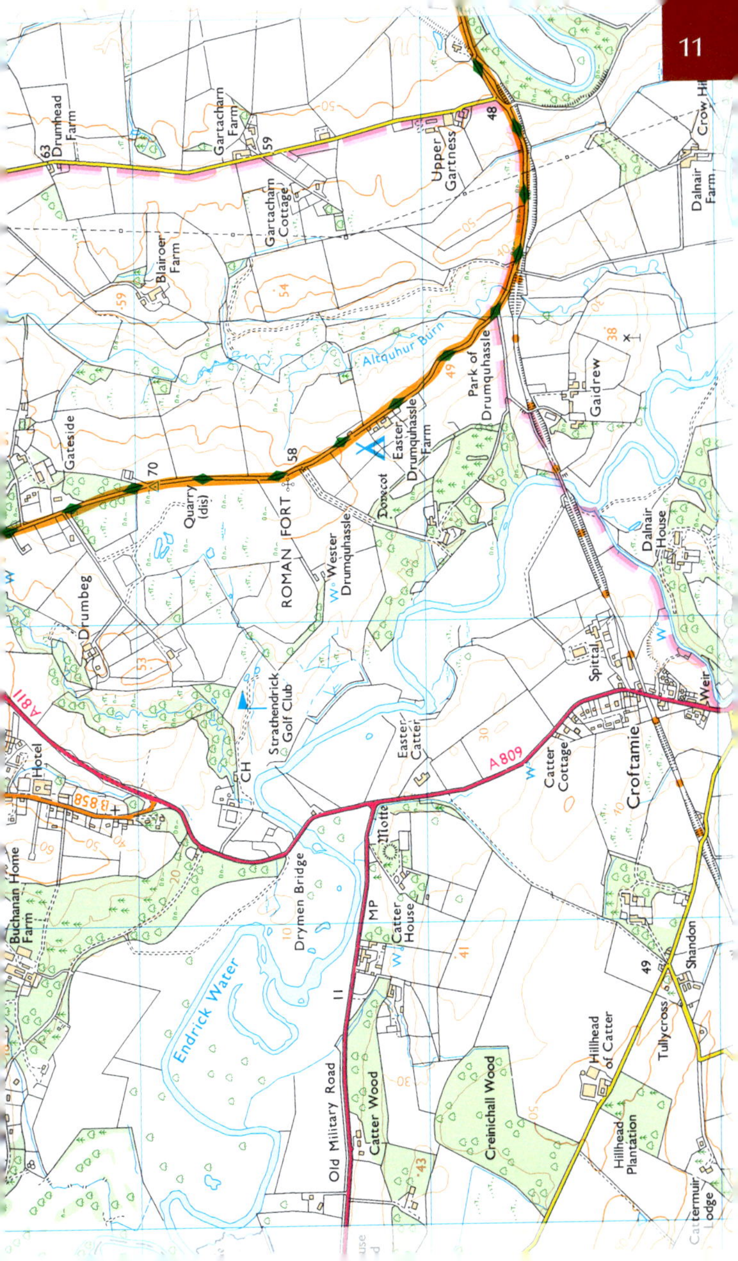

Drumhead Farm
Gartacharn Farm
Upper Gartness
Crow Hill
Dalnair Farm
Gartacharn Cottage
Blairoer Farm
Altquhur Burn
Park of Drumquhassle
Gaidrew
Gateside
Easter Drumquhassle Farm
Dovecot
Quarry (dis)
ROMAN FORT
Wester Drumquhassle
Dalnair House
Drumbeg
Strathendrick Golf Club
Spittal
Weir
A811
Hotel
B 858
CH
Easter Catter
A 809
Catter Cottage
Croftamie
Motte
Drymen Bridge
Buchanan Home Farm
MP
Catter House
Endrick Water
Shandon
Tullycross
Hillhead of Catter
Old Military Road
Catter Wood
Creinichall Wood
Hillhead Plantation
Cattermuir Lodge

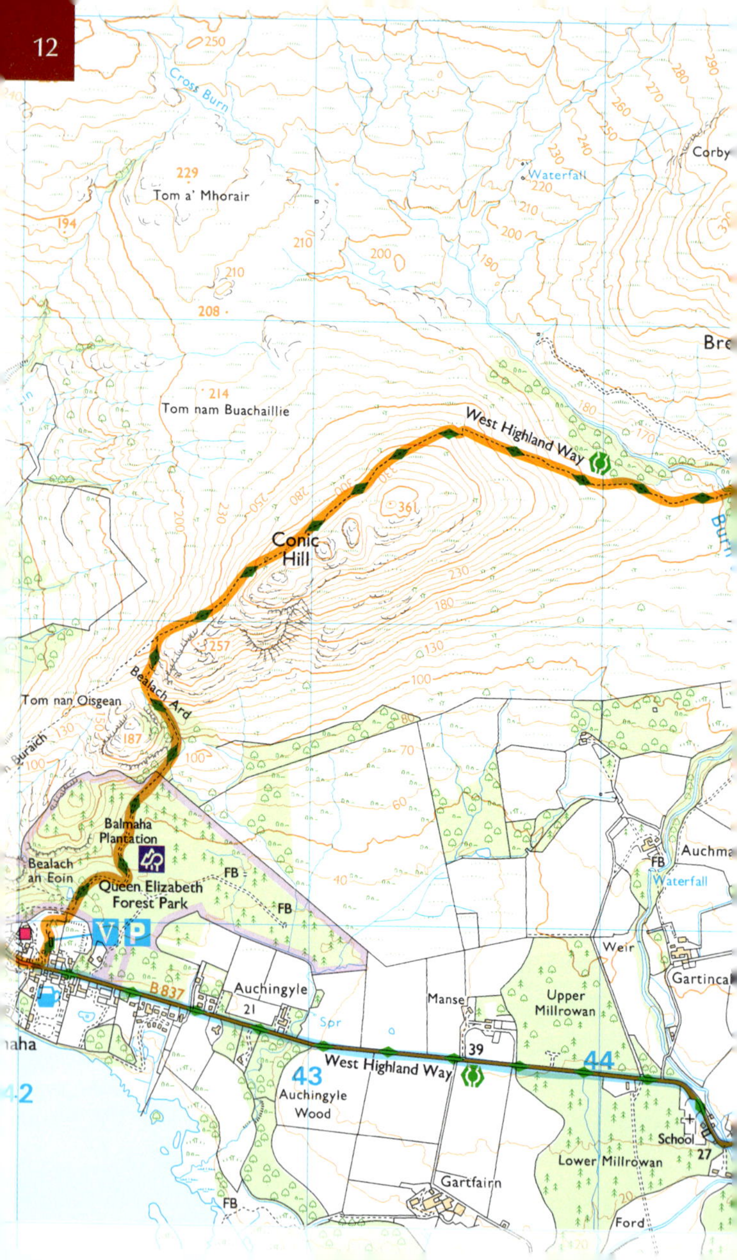
Cross Burn
Tom a' Mhorair
Waterfall
Corby
Tom nam Buachaillie
West Highland Way
Conic Hill
Bealach Ard
Tom nan Oisgean
Burn
Balmaha Plantation
Bealach an Eoin
Queen Elizabeth Forest Park
FB
Auchma
Waterfall
Weir
Gartinca
Auchingyle
Manse
Upper Millrowan
Spr
West Highland Way
Auchingyle Wood
Lower Millrowan
School
Gartfairn
Ford
42
43
44

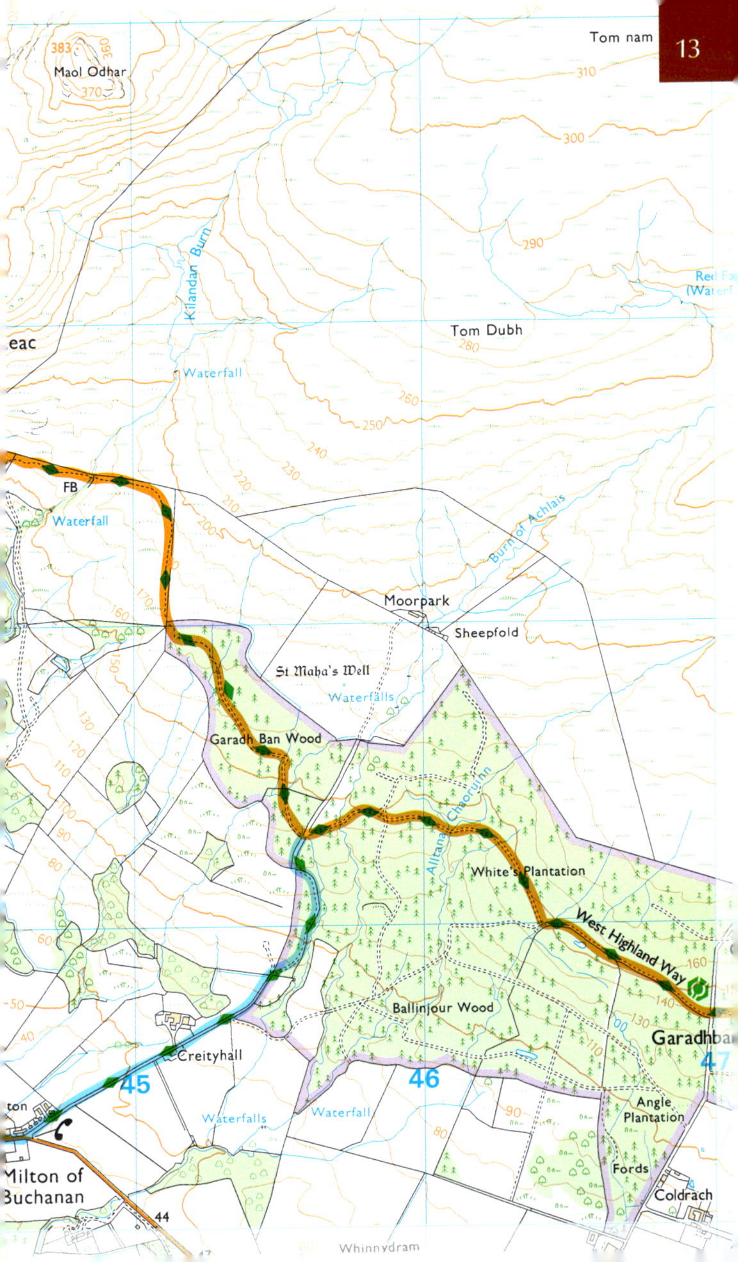
Tom nam
383
360
Maol Odhar
370
310
300
290
Red Fa
(Waterf
Kilandan Burn
Tom Dubh
280
eac
Waterfall
260
250
240
230
220
210
200
FB
Waterfall
Burn of Achlais
170
160
Moorpark
Sheepfold
150
St Maha's Well
Waterfalls
130
120
110
Garadh Ban Wood
Alltan a' Chaoruinn
100
90
80
White's Plantation
West Highland Way
160
140
130
60
50
Ballinjour Wood
Garadhba
47
40
Creityhall
45
46
110
ton
Waterfalls
Waterfall
90
Angle Plantation
80
Milton of Buchanan
Fords
Coldrach
44
Whinnydram

Ford
Blair Burn
Tom an Eagail
259
Creag Liath
187
Fords
Waterfalls
194
Allt Lin
Milarrochy
Creag Odhar
Cashell Glen
Cashell Burn
95
94
93
Ford
Blair
W H Way
Slipways
Basin
Weir
MS
Ardyle Wood
FB
Cashel Farm
27
Lag an Amair Wood
Queen Elizabeth Forest Park
Critreoch
Cnoc Buidhe
Strathcashell
Crannog
Fort
Strathcashell Point
Sheepfold
Badach Cragan
Anchorage Cottage
Jetty
Sallochy
Carn na Muice
Cnoc na Goibhre
62
Inchlonaig
Jetty

Balmaha
Jetties
Ferry P
Pier
Craigie Fort
Pass of Balmaha
Old Manse
Druim nam Buraich
Ford
Colle Ghlas
Arrochymore
Sheepfold
Janet's Burn
34
17
Dun (remains of)
Creag Mhòr
Arrochymore Point
The Kitchen Crannog
Inchcailloch
Tom na Nigheanan
Church (remains of)
Port Bawn
Pier
Jetty
Inchfad
Ellanderroch
Ceardach
Bucinch
Inchcruin
Jetty
42
41
40
39
38
92
91
90

Rowardennan to Crianlarich
Start Rowardennan
Finish Crianlarich
Distance 20 miles (32.5km)
Walking time 10–12hr
Cattle Grid
Sheepfold
Rowchnock
Tom Beithe
Rowardennan Lodge
Ardess
Ardess Burn
Rowardennan
Creaga Caorach
Creagan Breac
FB
Meml
Pier
Eilean nan Deargannan
Rowardennan Hotel
Port na Craoibhe
Rowardennan Forest
Stob Biorach
Coille Mhor Hill
Sheepfold
Cluan
Wood Burn
Caol Ghleann
Tom Mòr
Elrig
442
255
234

Lochan Maoil Dhuinne
Carraig
Coille Mhòr
Blairvockie
Cairn
Creag Mhor
FB
Mill of Ross
Crannog (submerged)
Rubha Fhuar a' Chos
Toman Lochain
Ross
W H Way
Dubh Loch Cottage
Dùn Maoil
Queen Elizabeth Forest Park
Dùn Mòr
Ford
FBs
Ben Lo
National Me
Quarry (dis)
Sallochy Wood
Dubh Lochan
Pilot Bay
Ross Wood
Boat House
Teac a' Mhinisteir
Sallochy Fo
Allt a Mhuilinn
Wester Sallochy
Allt a Mhorair
Ross Point
Camas an Losgainn
Dallurgan Burn
Port nam Ban
Sallochy
Culag
A 82
P

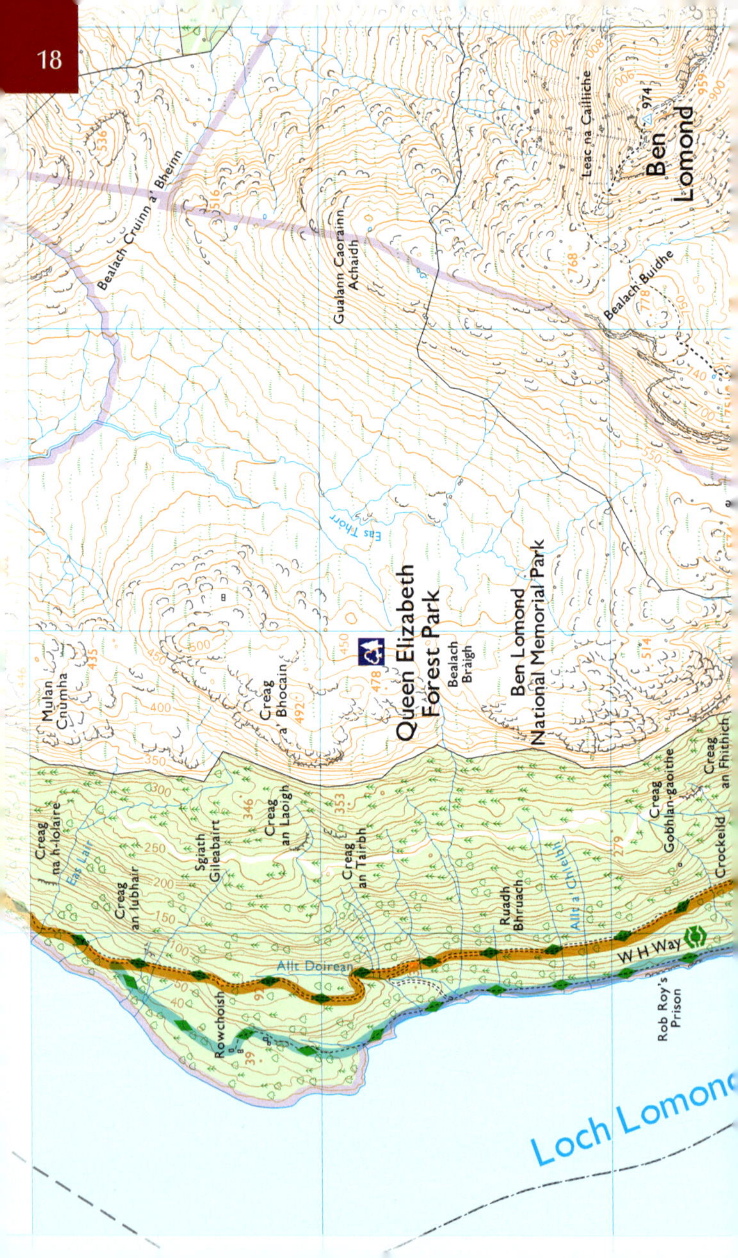
Ben Lomond
974
Leac na Cailliche
Bealach Buidhe
768
778
Bealach Cruinn a' Bheinn
536
516
Gualann Caorainn Achaidh
Eas Thorr
Queen Elizabeth Forest Park
Bealach Bràigh
Ben Lomond National Memorial Park
Mulan Cnumha
435
Creag a' Bhocain
492
478
500
514
Creag na h-Iolaire
Eas Lair
Creag an Iubhair
Sgiath Gileabairt
346
Creag an Laoigh
353
Creag an Tairbh
Ruadh Bhruach
Allt a' Chlebh
279
Creag Gobhlan-gaoithe
Creag an Fhithich
Crockeild
Allt Doirean
Rowchoish
39
W H Way
Rob Roy's Prison
Loch Lomond

Coire Odhar
Ptarmigan
Bealach
Tom Fithich
Spùt Bàn
Cattle
West Highland Way
Allt Garbh
Snegain
Eas
Ptarmigan Lodge
Creag an Leat
Creag Iolaire
The Yett of Ptarmigan
Rubha Curraichd
a' Bhruic
Ferry P
(Summer)
Firkin Point
Firkin
Firkin Burn
MP
P
Rubha Mòr
A 82
Rubha Dubh
Rubha Ban
Old Military Road
Robert the Bruce's Tree
Stùc an t-Iobairt
Allt Stùc an t-Iobairt
12
13
33
34
35
36
37

Inversnaid Lodge
Weir
FB
93
23
Inversnaid Hotel
Piers
Falls
FBs
Great Trossachs Path
Clach Buidhe
180
Ford
WH Way
Maol Reamhar
350
390
380
Waterfalls
430
Coire Fearna
536
Fords
Ashlan
Cruachan
Creag Ashlan
490
Waterfall
Lochan Cruachan
30
50
100
150
200
250
300
350
400
450
500
Creag an Daraich
Waterfalls
Stuickiruagh
FB
Waterfalls
Easan Dubh
Sgorr a' Chait
350
Cailness
Loch Lom
FB
332
Tigh na Stuichd
Fords
Ford
Craig Royston
Cailness Bu
Cnap Mòr
370
Ford
Ford
Creag an Achaidh Fearna
382
446
Isle
Creag

Island
I Vow
Castle
(remains of)
10
Ford
West Highland Way
Allt Rostan
Creag Ca
Cnap nan Garradh
Ford
rough
Ceann Mòr
Creag
an Fhithich
Ardvorlich
Cottage
15
Pollochro Burn
Pollochro
Tom na
h-Innse
MS
Inversnaid
Nature Reserve
300
250
12
200
18
Snaid Burn
an Arnain
150
50
33
34
35
Sheepfold
150
Sroin
Uaidh
Rob Roy's Cave
150
Leacainn
Iasgair
FB
Ford
Inversnaid
210
200
170
150
Cladachbeag
Boat House
FBs
Arklet Water
Ferry P
Binnein
116
140
Inversnaid
Lodge
Weir
Fall
FB
93

Ford
Dubh Lochan
Fords
164
Cnap Mor
97
Cruach
514
400
450
500
Pontoons
Ford
Ardlui
Ardleish
Ferry P (Summer)
Landing Stage
Landing Stage
FB
150
200
300
400
450
Lochan nam Muc
Fords
Burnside Cottage
21
A82
Ford
Ford
Ford
Cairn
Stuckendroin
Fords
Doune
Ford
Loch Lomond
Creag an Fhithich
Stob Eighr
613
11
MS
Creag a' Mhadaidh
70
Ford
Clach nan Tarbh or Pulpit Rock
16
Tom Dubh
FBs
Sheep Creep
Meall an t-Seabhaig
Smuggler's Cave
Sheep Creep
Creag a' Phuirt
Rubha Ban
50
150
250
350
450
500
600

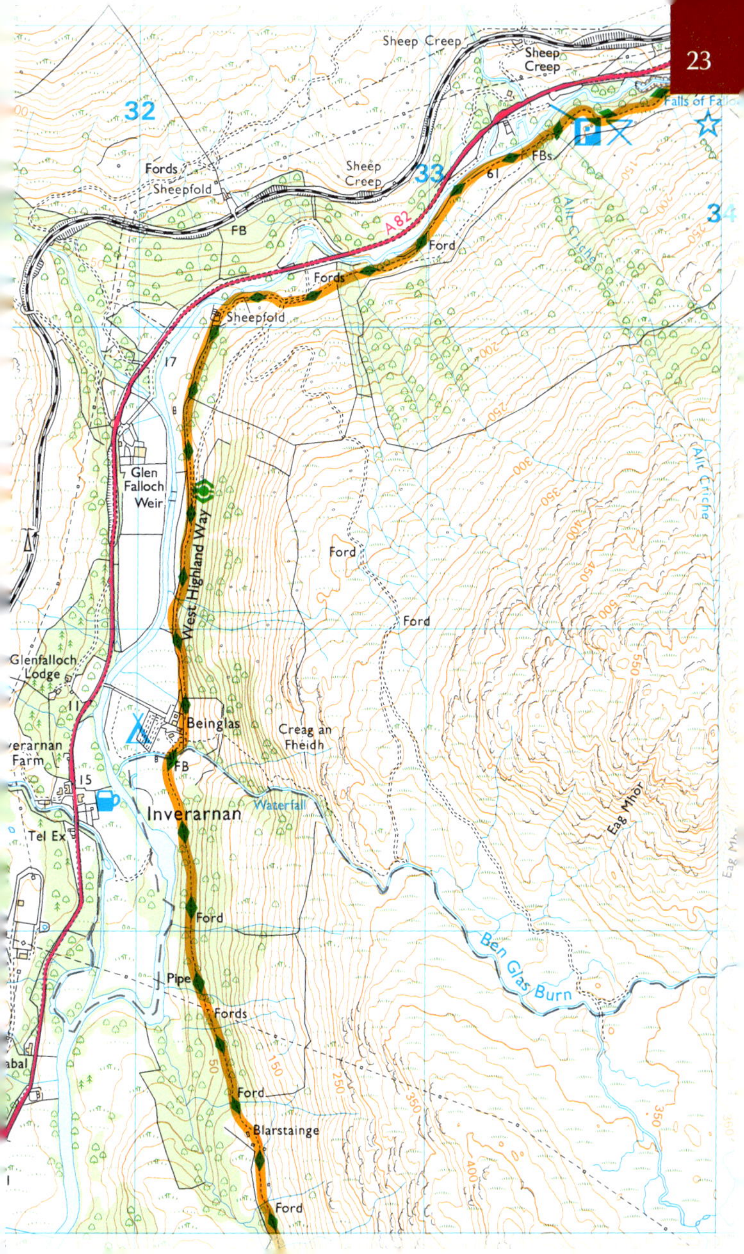
Sheep Creep
Sheep Creep
Falls of Falloch
32
33
34
Fords
Sheepfold
Sheep Creep
FB
FBs
61
A82
Ford
Fords
Sheepfold
Allt Criche
17
200
250
300
350
400
450
500
550
Glen Falloch Weir
West Highland Way
Ford
Ford
Allt Criche
Glenfalloch Lodge
11
Beinglas
Creag an Fheidh
Inverarnan Farm
FB
15
Inverarnan
Waterfall
Eag Mhor
Tel Ex
Ford
Ben Glas Burn
Pipe
Fords
50
150
250
350
Ford
Blarstainge
400
350
Ford

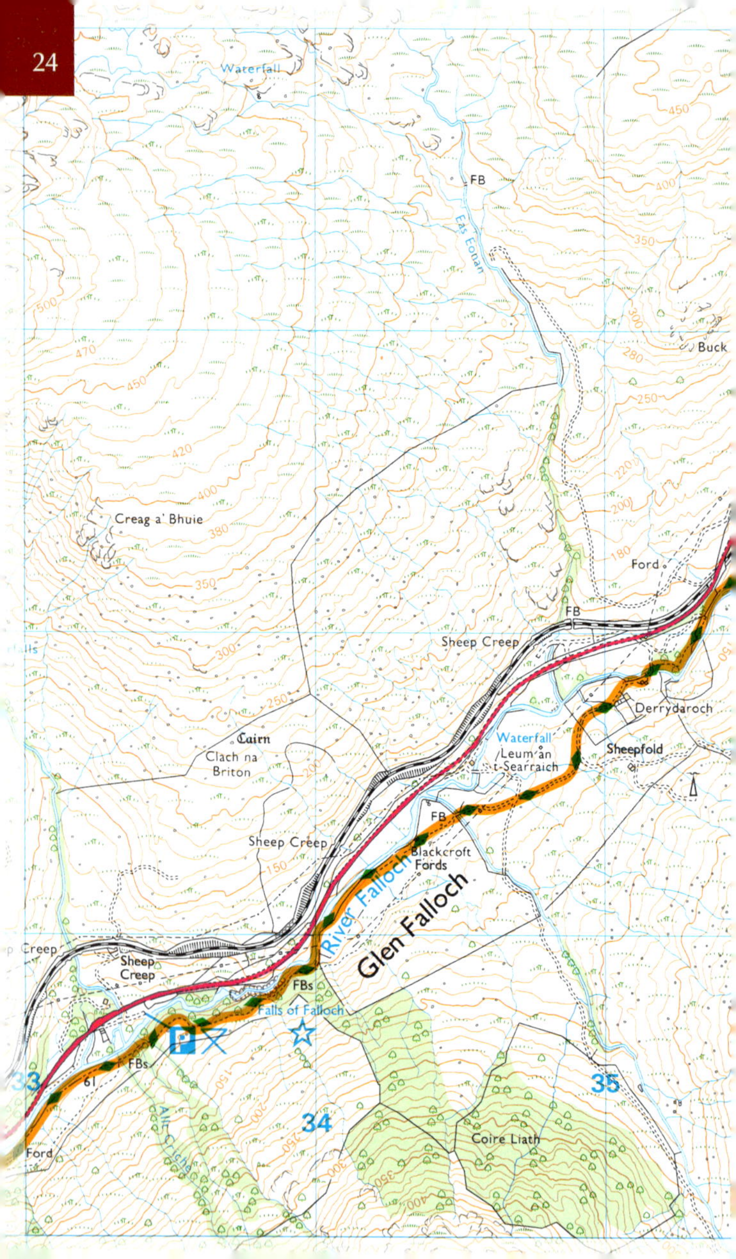
Waterfall
FB
Eas Eonan
Buck
Creag a' Bhuie
Ford
FB
Sheep Creep
Derrydaroch
Cairn
Clach na Briton
Waterfall
Leum an t-Searraich
Sheepfold
FB
Sheep Creep
Blackcroft Fords
River Falloch
Glen Falloch
Creep
Sheep Creep
FBs
Falls of Falloch
FBs
61
33
34
35
Allt Criche
Coire Liath
Ford

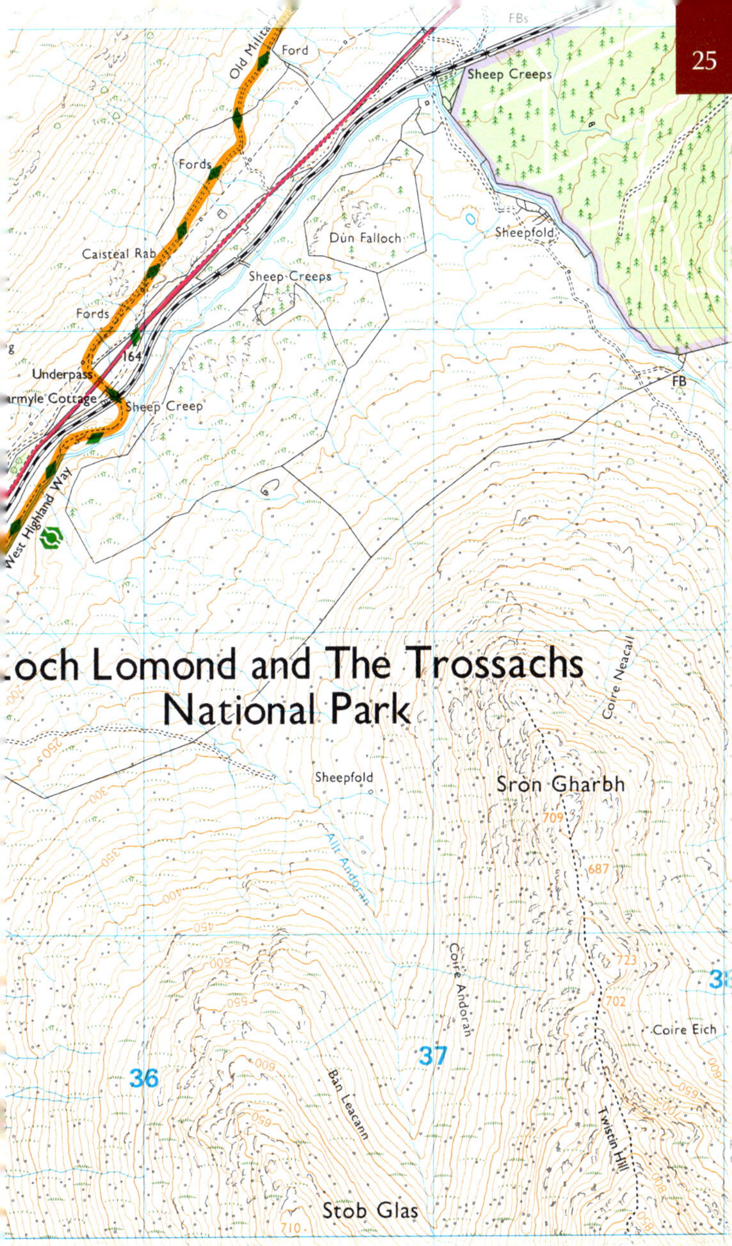
FBs
Ford
Old Military
Sheep Creeps
Fords
Dun Falloch
Sheepfold
Caisteal Rab
Sheep Creeps
Fords
164
Underpass
rmyle Cottage
Sheep Creep
FB
West Highland Way
Loch Lomond and The Trossachs
National Park
Coire Neacail
Sheepfold
Sron Gharbh
709
687
Allt Andoran
Coire Andoran
723
702
Coire Eich
37
36
Ban Leacann
Twistin Hill
Stob Glas
710

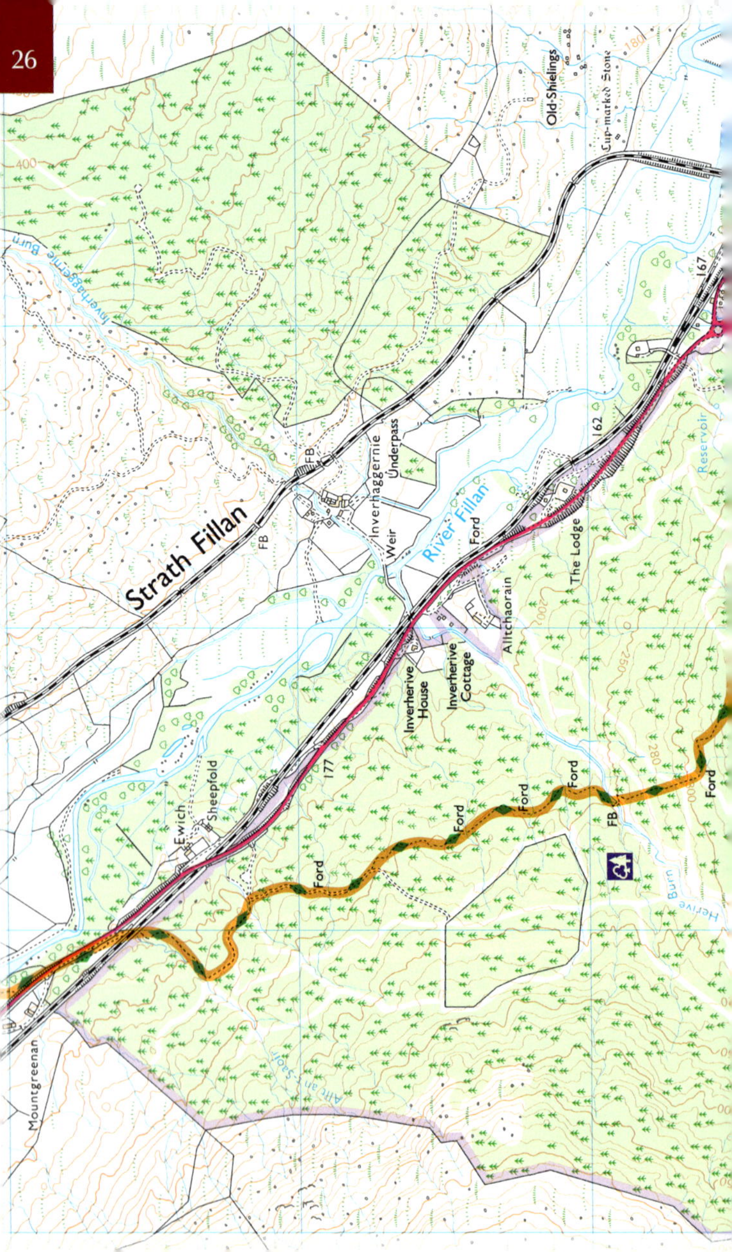
Strath Fillan
River Fillan
Inverhaggernie Burn
Inverhaggernie
Underpass
Weir
FB
Ford
Alltchaorain
The Lodge
Inverherive House
Inverherive Cottage
Ewich
Sheepfold
Mountgreenan
Old Shielings
Cup-marked Stone
Reservoir
Herive Burn
Allt an t-Saoir
162
167
177

Crianlarich to Bridge of Orchy

Start Crianlarich
Finish Bridge of Orchy
Distance 13½ miles (21.5km)
Walking time 7hr

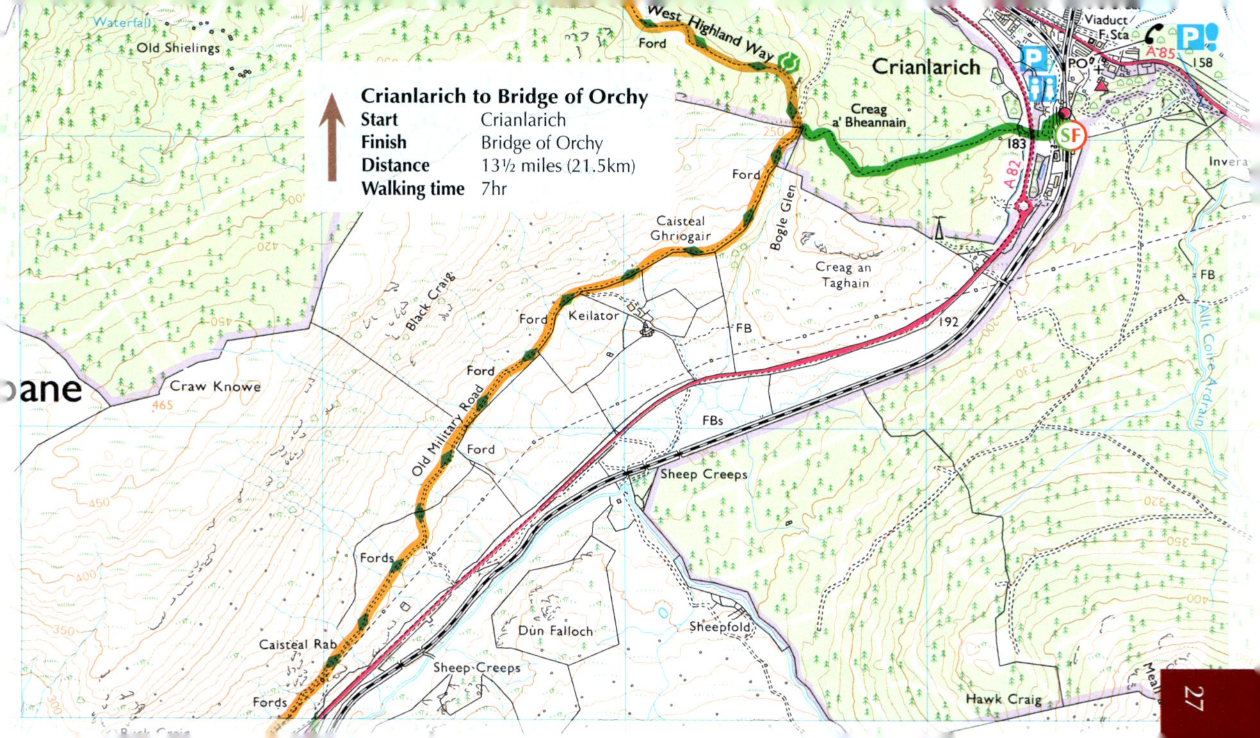

Beinn Chaorach
Caol Ghleann
Sheepfold
Old
Allt a' Chaol Ghlinne
35
Meall Buidhe
Cairn
653
603
Creagan Gaothach
Creagan Glas
Sheepfold
Meml
Dam
Crom Allt
Old Military Road
West Highland Way
MS
306
291
Cemy
Tighness
Hotel
33
PO
Clifton
A 82
247
Lead Mine
32
(dis)

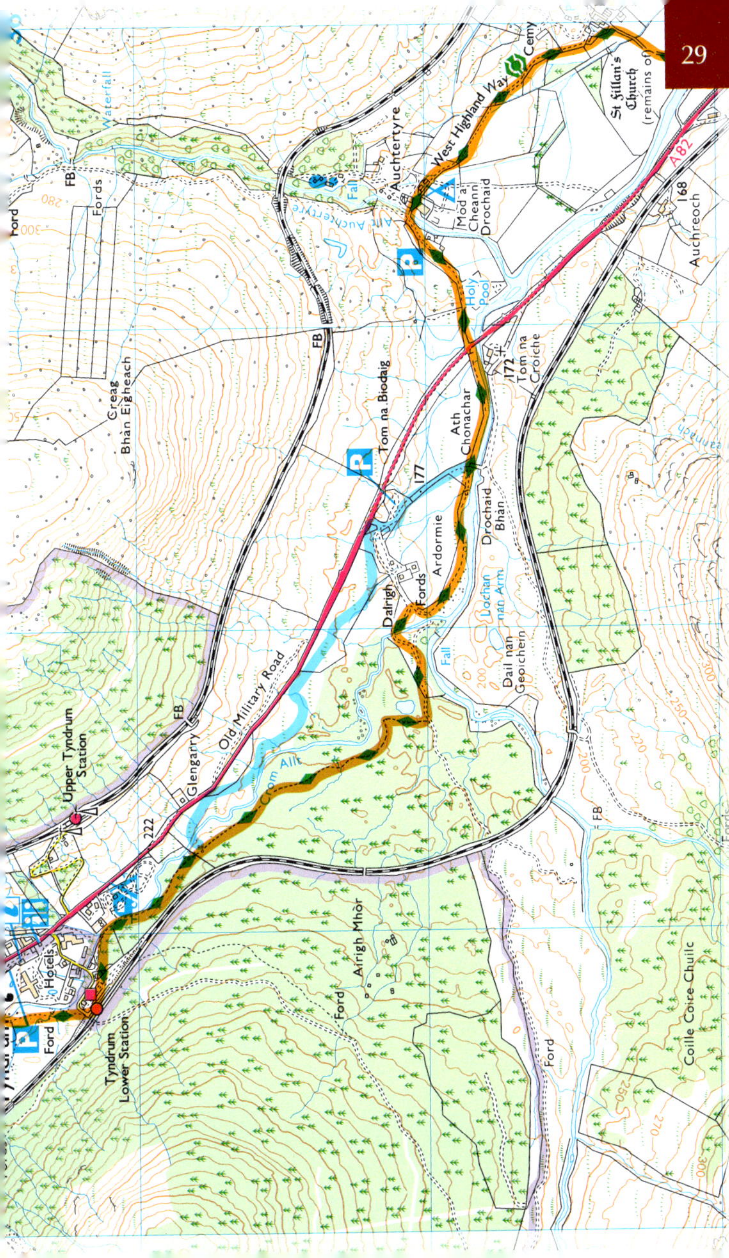

Waterfall
FB
Fords
Ford
280
300
Creag Bhàn Eigheach
FB
Old Military Road
Glengarry
FB
Upper Tyndrum Station
222
Hotels
Ford
Tyndrum Lower Station
Airigh Mhòr
Ford
Crom Allt
Dalrigh
Fords
Ardormie
Tom na Biodaig
177
Ath Chonachar
Drochaid Bhàn
Lochan nan Arm
Fall
Dail nan Geoichein
200
172
Tom na Croiche
Holy Pool
Allt Auchtertyre
Fall
Auchtertyre
West Highland Way
Mòd a' Cheann Drochaid
Cemy
St Fillan's Church (remains of)
A82
168
Auchreoch
250
300
220
200
FB
Fords
Ford
Coille Coire Chuilc
250
270
300

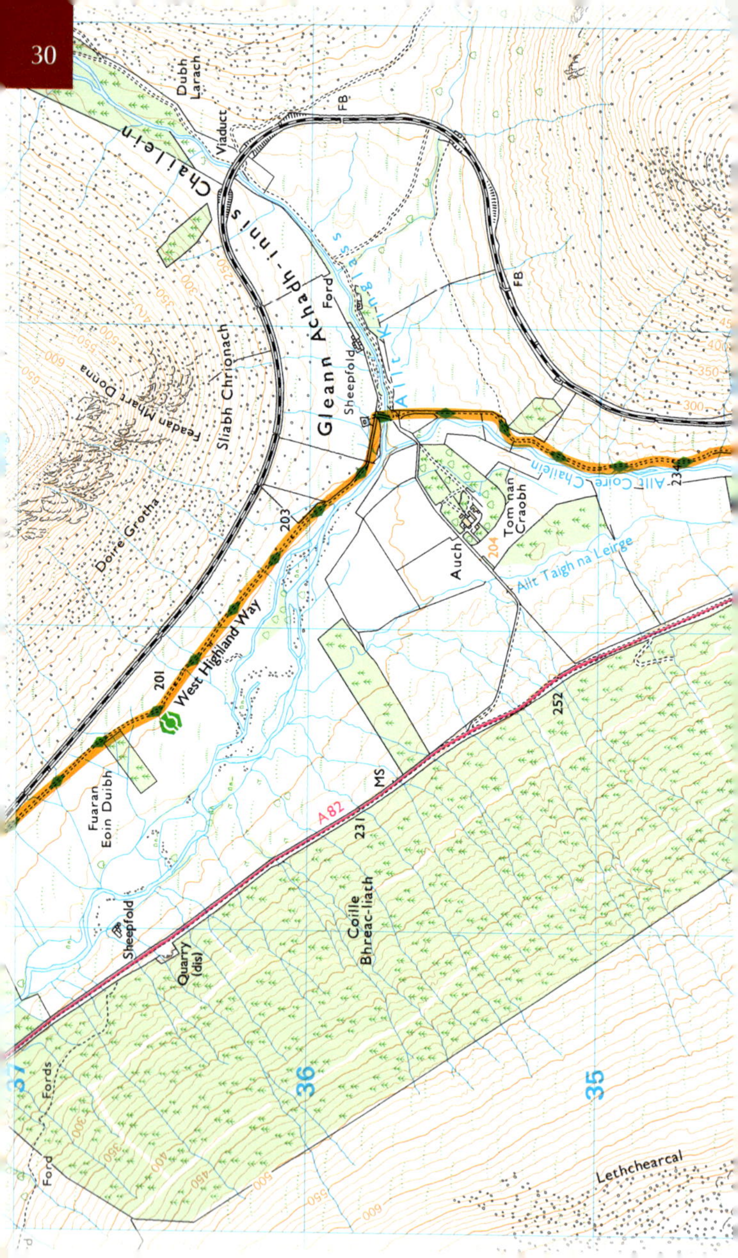

Dubh Larach
Viaduct
FB
Gleann Achadh-innis Chailein
Sliabh Chrionach
Feadan Mhart Donna
Doire Grotha
Ford
Sheepfold
Allt Kinglass
FB
Allt Coire Chailein
Tom nan Craobh
Auch
Allt Taigh na Leirge
West Highland Way
Fuaran Eoin Duibh
MS
A82
Coille Bhreac-liath
Quarry (dis)
Sheepfold
Fords
Ford
Lethchearcal
203
201
204
234
252
231
37
36
35

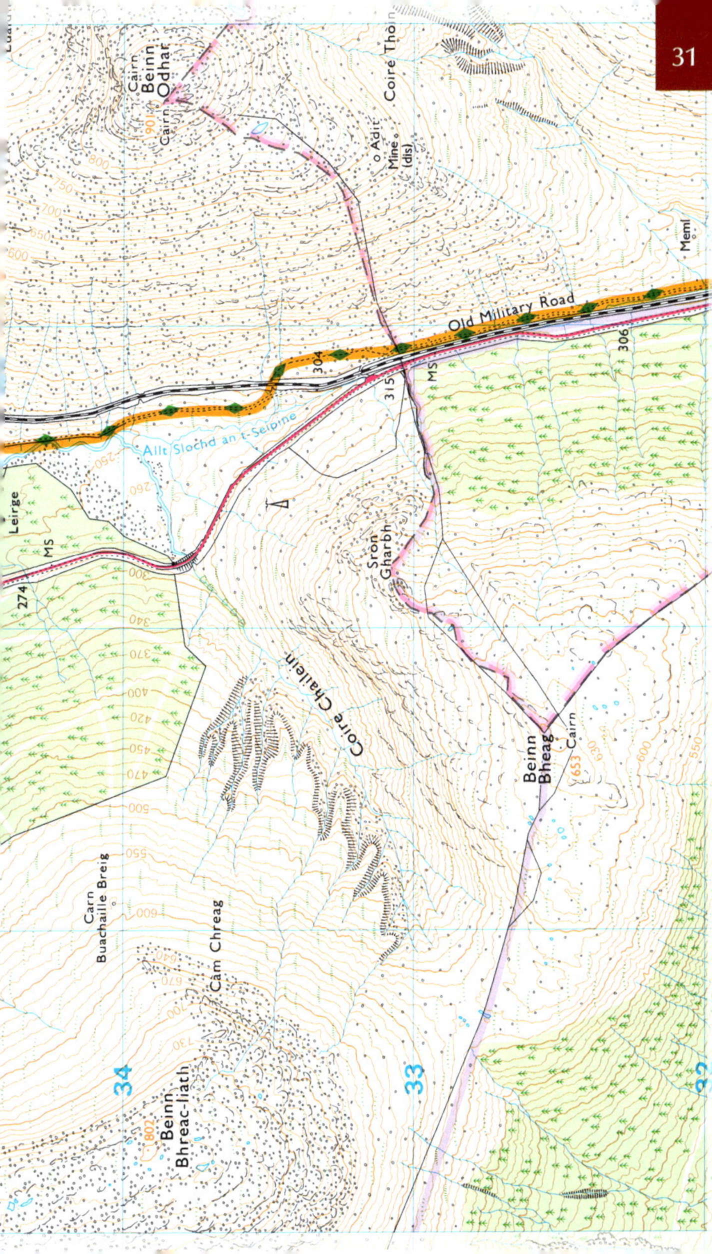

Beinn Odhar
Cairn
901
Coire Tho
Adit
Mine (dis)
Meml
Old Military Road
304
315
MS
306
Allt Slochd an t-Seipine
Leirge
MS
274
Sron Gharbh
Coire Chailein
Beinn Bheag
Cairn
653
Carn Buachaille Breig
Càm Chreag
Beinn Bhreac-liath
802
34
33
32

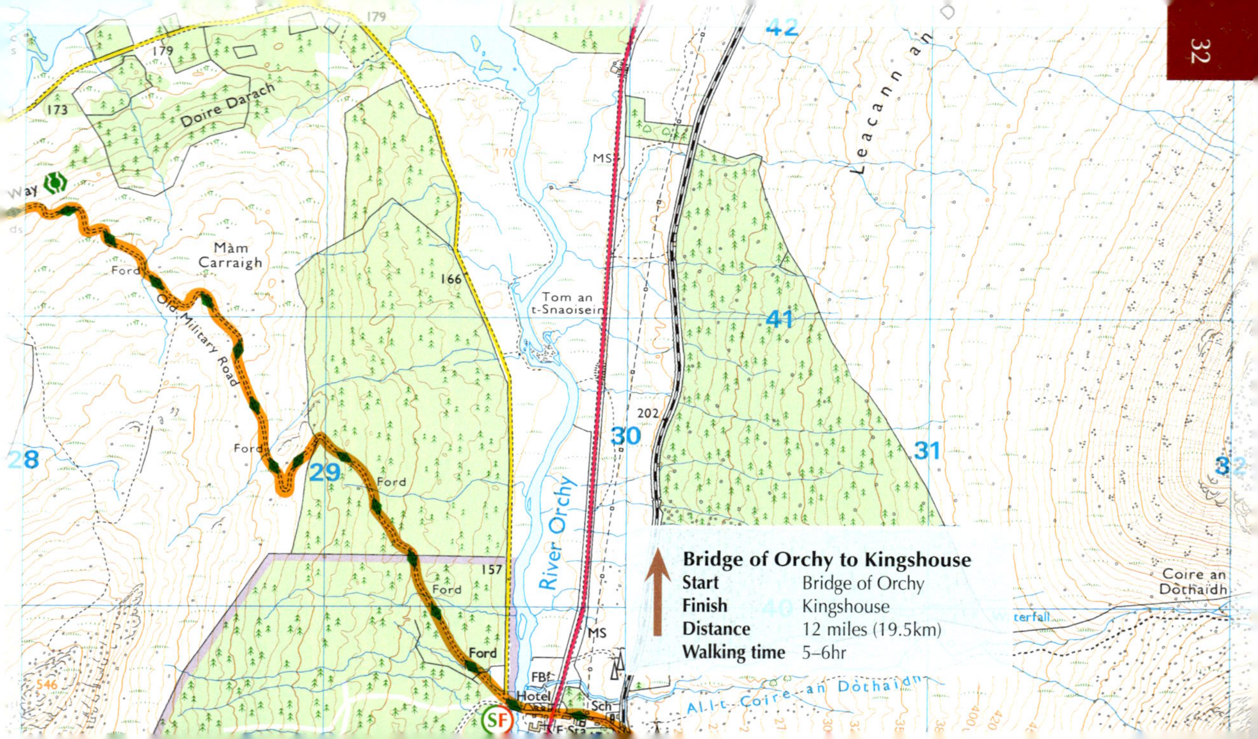

Bridge of Orchy to Kingshouse

Start	Bridge of Orchy
Finish	Kingshouse
Distance	12 miles (19.5km)
Walking time	5–6hr

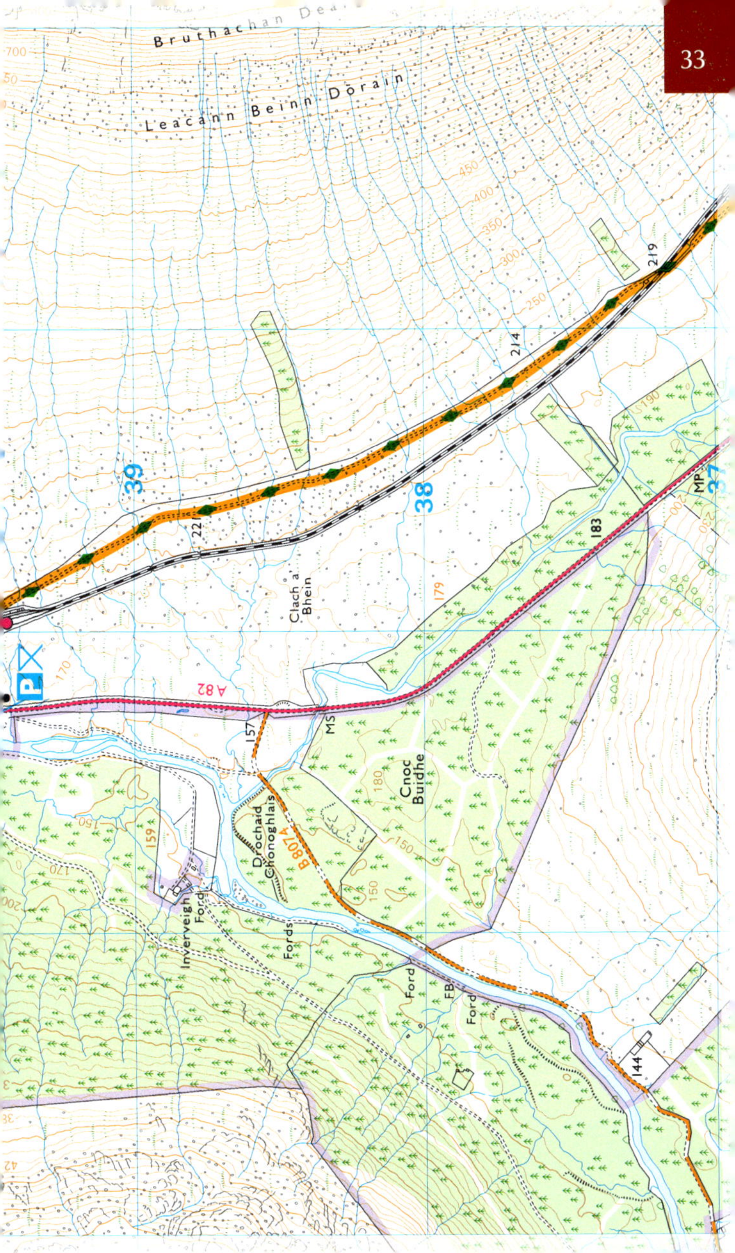
Bruthachan Dea
Leacann Beinn Dòrain
700
450
400
350
300
250
219
214
221
39
38
37
MP
183
179
190
200
230
Clach a' Bhein
P
170
A 82
157
MS
Cnoc Buidhe
180
150
Drochaid Chonoghlais
B8074
159
150
170
200
Inverveigh
Ford
Fords
Ford
FB
Ford
144

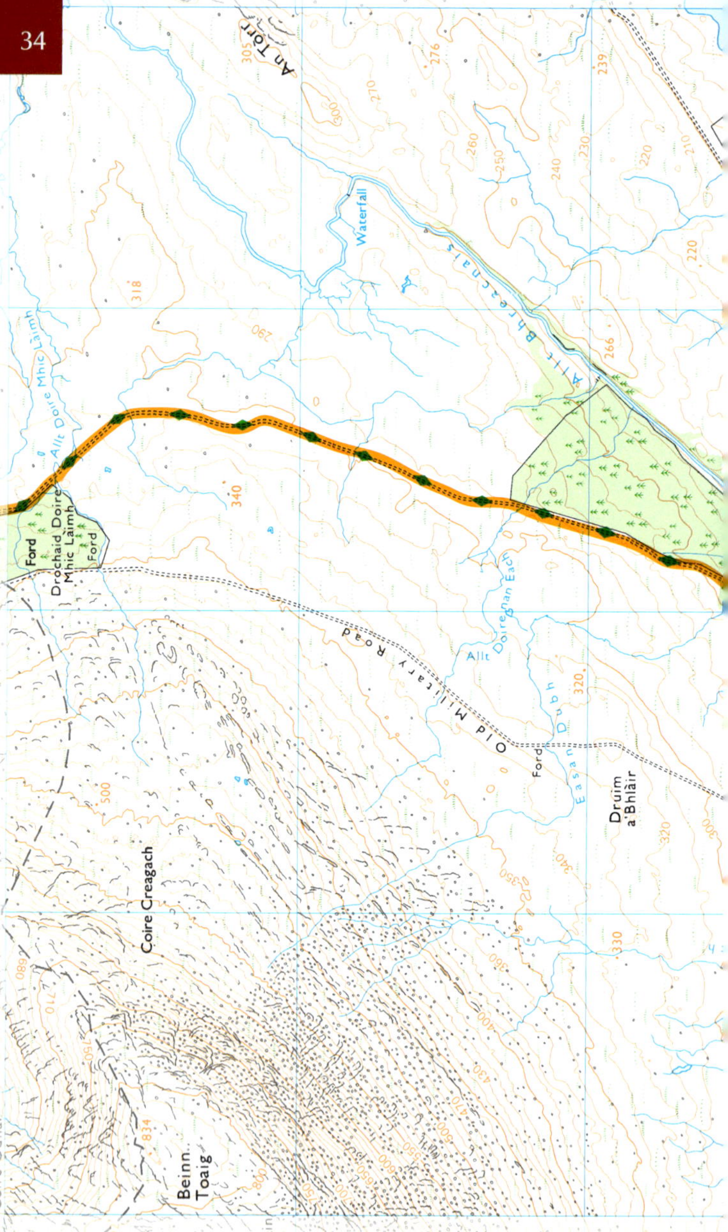
An Torr
Waterfall
Allt Bhreacnais
Allt Doire Mhic Làimh
Ford
Drochaid Doire Mhic Làimh
Ford
Old Military Road
Allt Doire nan Each
Easan Dubh
Ford
Druim a'Bhlàir
Coire Creagach
Beinn Toaig

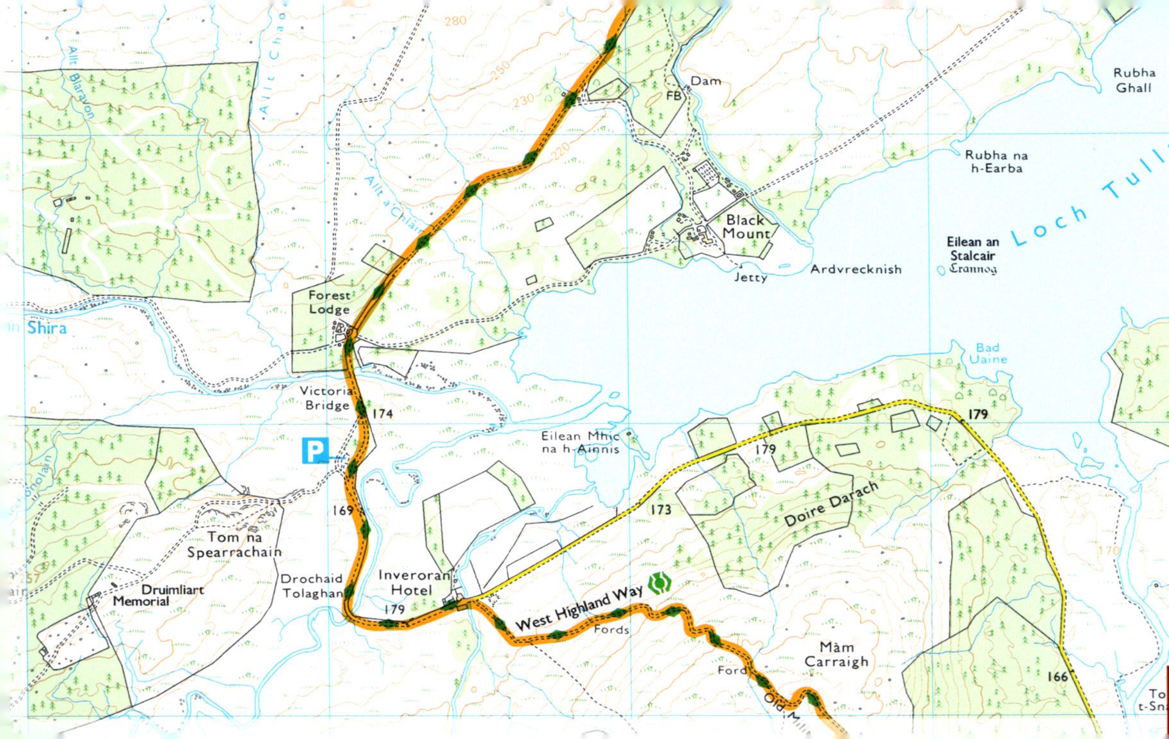
Loch Tulla
Rubha Ghall
Rubha na h-Earba
Eilean an Stalcair
Crannog
Ardvrecknish
Jetty
Black Mount
Dam
FB
Bad Uaine
Forest Lodge
Victoria Bridge
Shira
Allt Blaravon
Allt Chao
Allt a'Chlàin
Eilean Mhic na h-Ainnis
Inveroran Hotel
Drochaid Tolaghan
Tom na Spearrachain
Druimliart Memorial
West Highland Way
Fords
Ford
Doire Darach
Màm Carraigh
Old M
MS
179
174
169
173
166
188
170
220
230
250
280

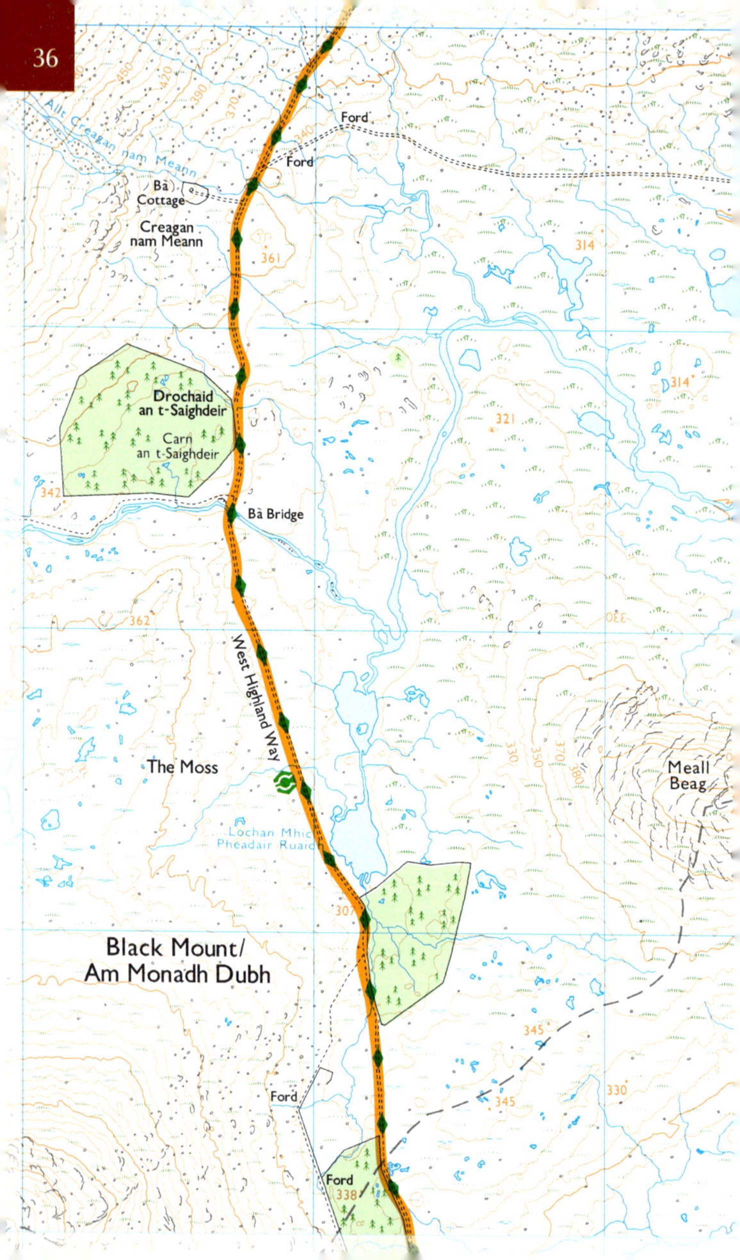
Allt Creagan nam Meann
Ford
Ford
Bà Cottage
Creagan nam Meann
361
314
Drochaid an t-Saighdeir
Carn an t-Saighdeir
321
314
342
Bà Bridge
362
330
West Highland Way
The Moss
Lochan Mhic Pheadair Ruaidh
330
350
370
380
Meall Beag
307
Black Mount/
Am Monadh Dubh
345
Ford
345
330
Ford
338
450
420
390
370
340

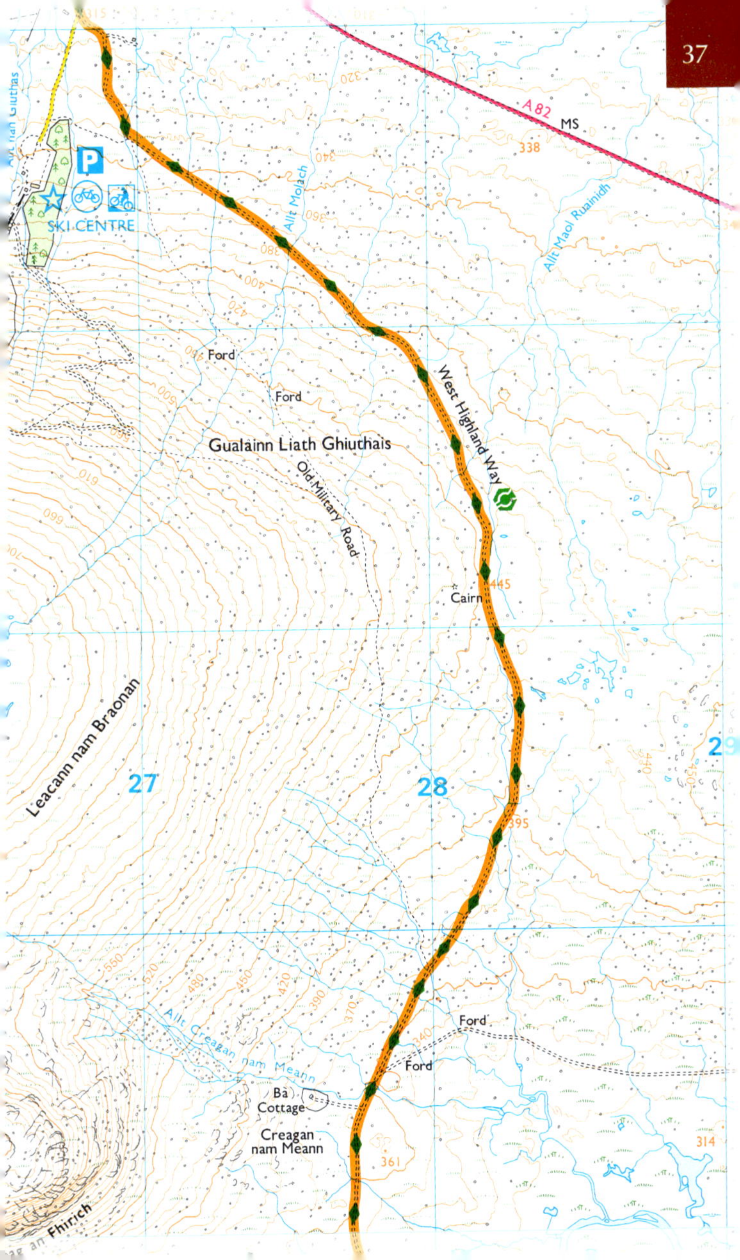
A82
MS
338
Allt Molach
Allt Maol Ruainidh
SKI CENTRE
Ford
Ford
Gualainn Liath Ghiuthais
Old Military Road
West Highland Way
Cairn
445
Leacann nam Braonan
27
28
395
Allt Creagan nam Meann
Ford
Ford
Bà Cottage
Creagan nam Meann
361
314
Fhirich

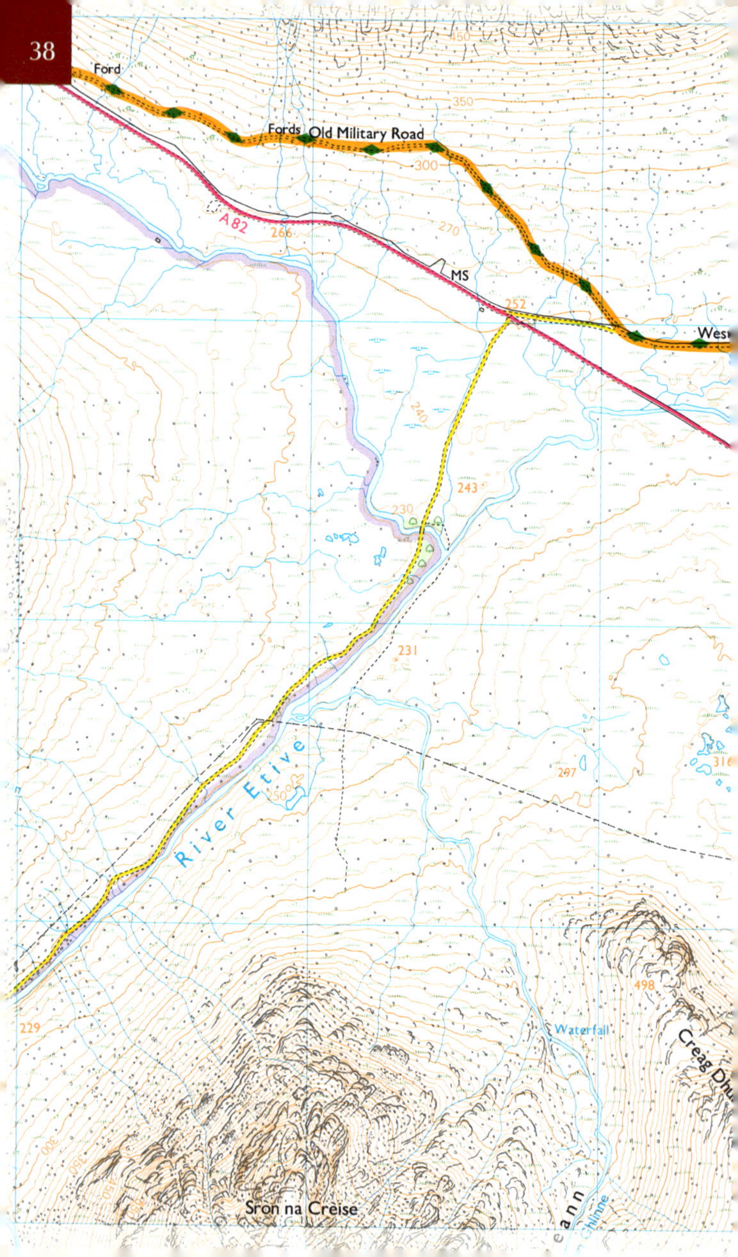
Ford
Fords
Old Military Road
450
350
300
270
A 82
266
MS
252
West
240
243
230
231
River Etive
250
297
316
498
229
300
350
450
Waterfall
Creag Dhu
Sron na Creise
Chlinne

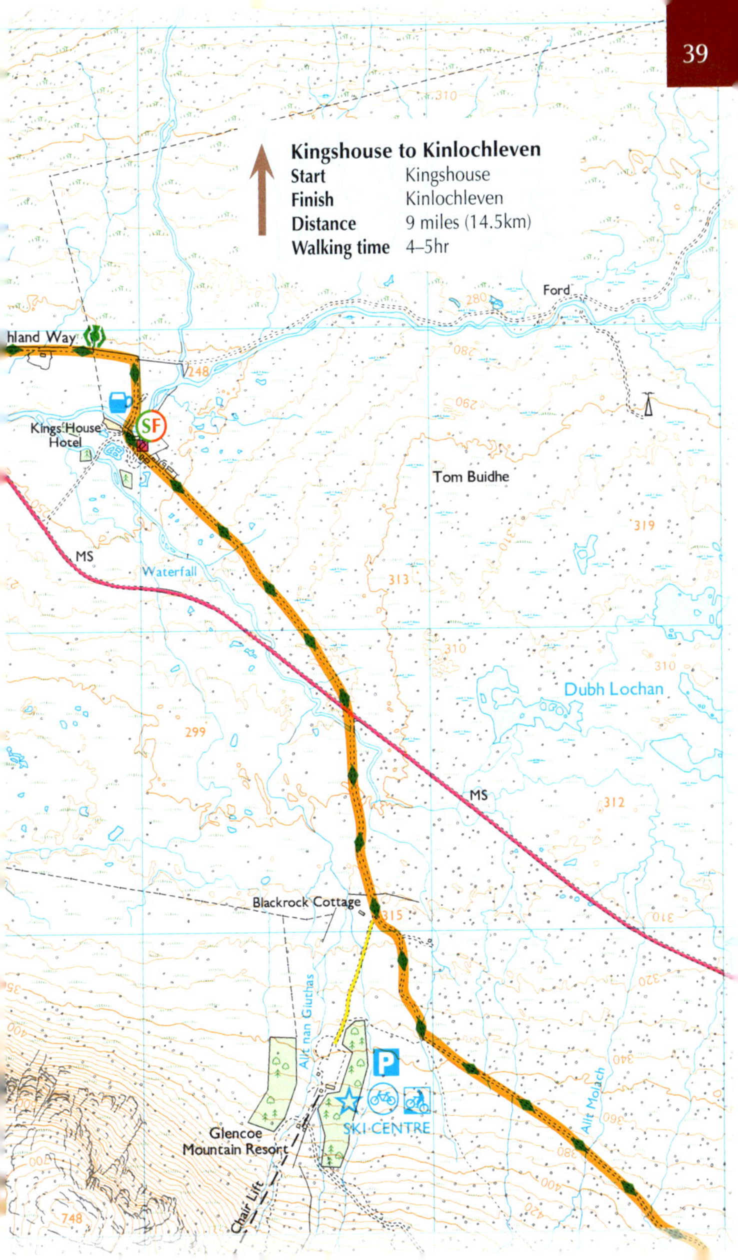
Kingshouse to Kinlochleven
Start Kingshouse
Finish Kinlochleven
Distance 9 miles (14.5km)
Walking time 4–5hr
hland Way
Kings House Hotel
SF
Ford
Tom Buidhe
MS
Waterfall
Dubh Lochan
Blackrock Cottage
Allt nan Giuthas
Allt Molach
SKI CENTRE
Glencoe Mountain Resort
Chair Lift

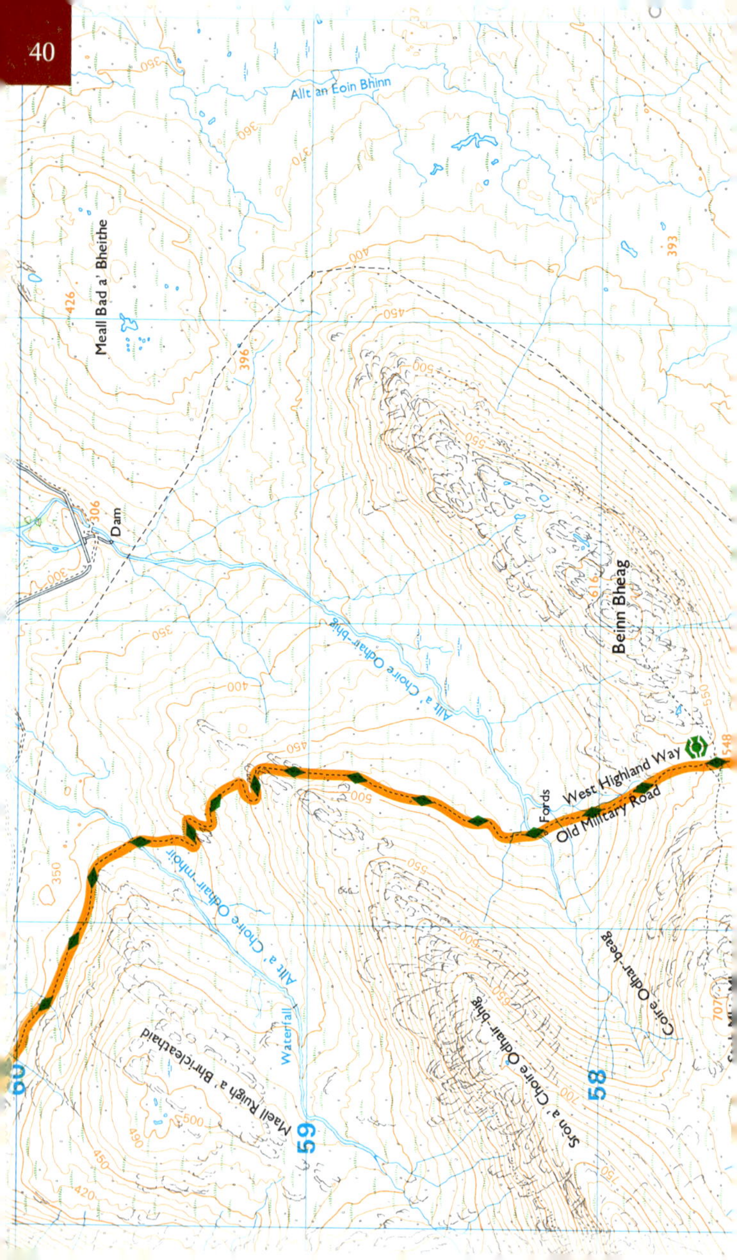
Allt an Eoin Bhinn
Meall Bad a' Bheithe
426
396
393
Dam
306
Beinn Bheag
616
Allt a' Choire Odhair-bhig
West Highland Way
Old Military Road
Fords
548
Allt a' Choire Odhair-mhoir
Waterfall
Maell Ruigh a' Bhricleathaid
Sron a' Choire Odhair-bhig
Coire Odhar-beag
707
60
59
58

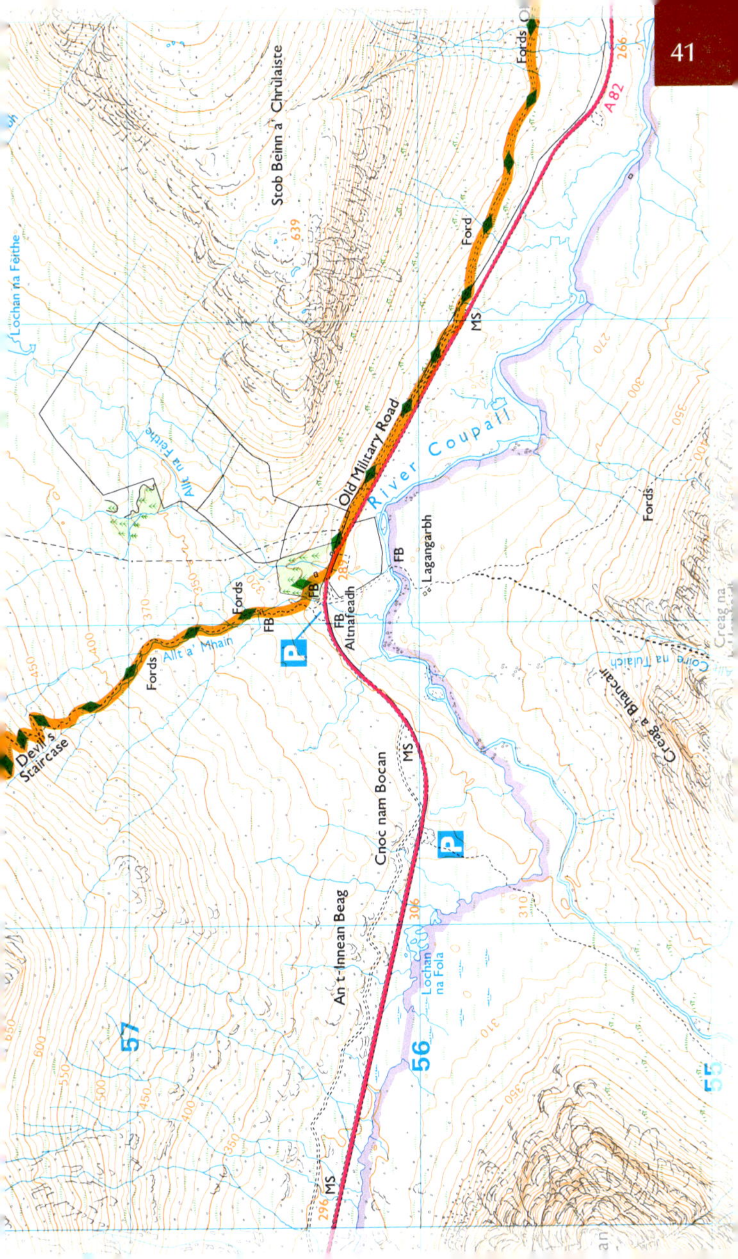
Devil's Staircase
Fords
Allt a' Mhain
FB
Altnafeadh
Old Military Road
River Coupall
Lagangarbh
Stob Beinn a' Chrulaiste
Lochan na Feithe
Allt na Feithe
Ford
MS
A82
Cnoc nam Bocan
An t-Innean Beag
Lochan na Fola
Creag a' Bhancair
Coire na Tulaich
57
56
55

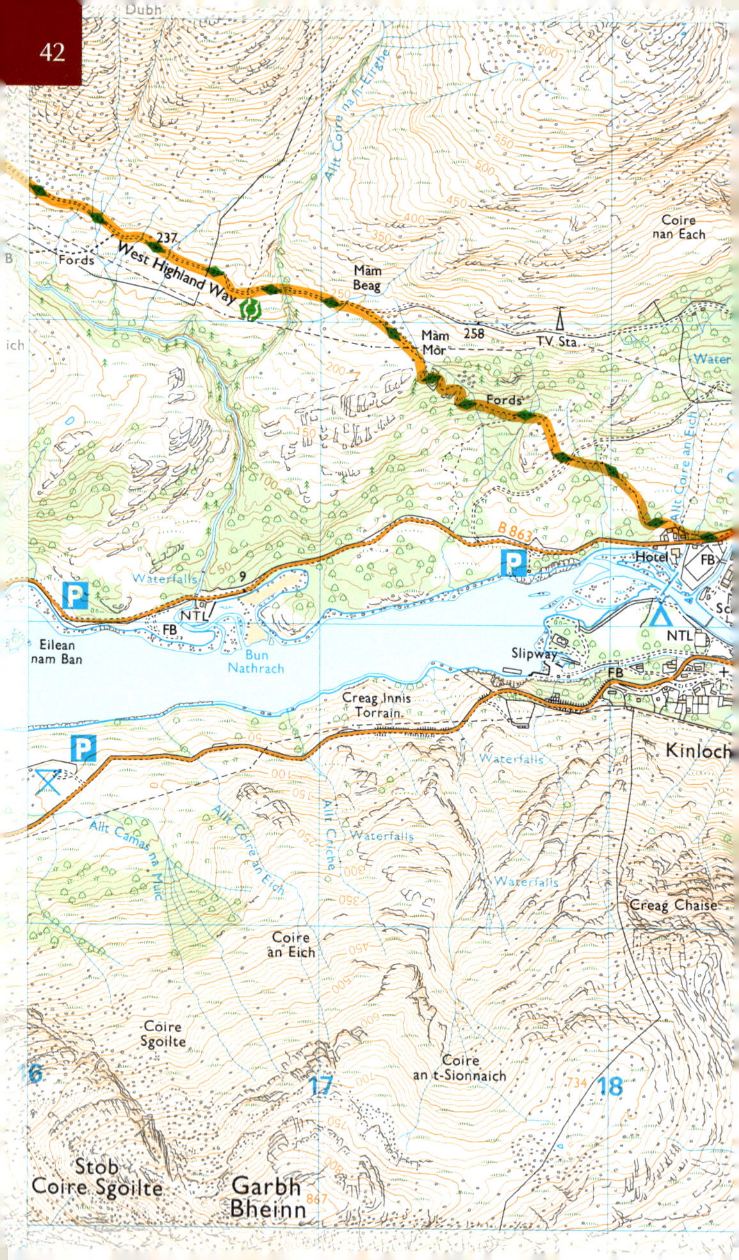
Dubh
Allt Coire na h-Eirghe
Coire nan Each
237
Fords
West Highland Way
Mam Beag
Mam Mor
258
TV Sta
Water
Fords
B 863
Hotel
FB
Waterfalls
NTL
FB
Eilean nam Ban
Bun Nathrach
Slipway
NTL
Creag Innis Torrain
FB
Kinloch
Waterfalls
Allt Camas na Muic
Allt Coire an Eich
Allt Criche
Waterfalls
Waterfalls
Creag Chaise
Coire an Eich
Coire Sgoilte
Coire an t-Sionnaich
734
17
18
Stob Coire Sgoilte
Garbh Bheinn
867

Kinlochleven to Fort William

Start	Kinlochleven
Finish	Fort William
Distance	15½ miles (25km)
Walking time	7–8hr

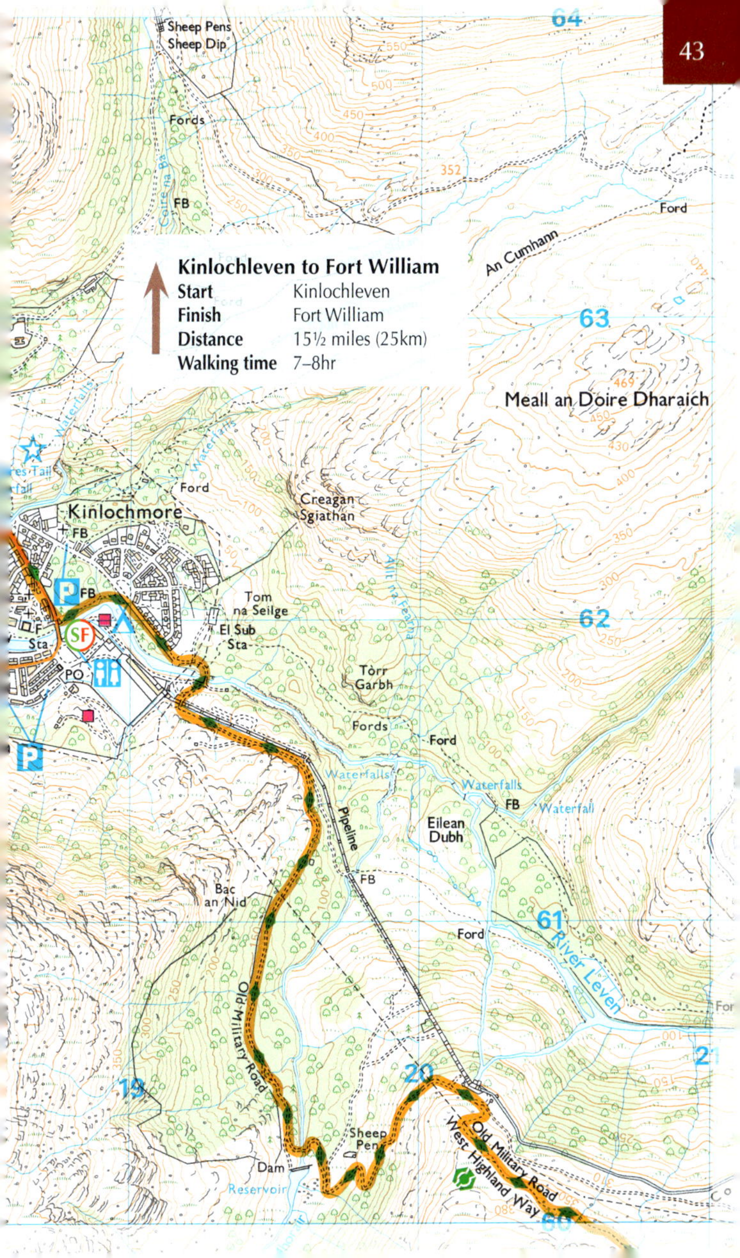

Allt a' Choire Charaich
Allt Coire na Sleubhaich
Tigh-na-sleubhaich
Sprs
Sprs
Fords
Fords
Sheepfold
Lairigmòr
(ruin)
FB
Old
Ford
Waterfall
Allt Fraoch Choire Mòr
Allt Fraoch Choire Beag
Fraoch
Choire
Loch
an Sgòir
Cairn
Beinn
na Caillich
Cairn
764
A' Chailleach
Allt na Caillich
Fords
Fords
Ford
Camas
Calltuinn
Cemy
Quarry
(dis)
Caolas nan Con
NTL
Camas Allt
a' Mhaim
Torr
a' Phloda

Coire a' Bhutha
Allt Coire a' Bhutha
Stob Coire na h-Eirghe
Coire Dubh
Road
Allt Nathrach
FB
Fords
West Highland Way
Meall na h-Oinsich
Lochaber
Allt a' Chaorainn
Allt na h-Oinsich
Waterfalls
Waterfall
NTL
FB
Camas Eilean nam Ban
Eilean nam Ban
Bun Nathrach
Camas na Muic
Allt Camas na Muic
Allt Coire an Eich
Coire

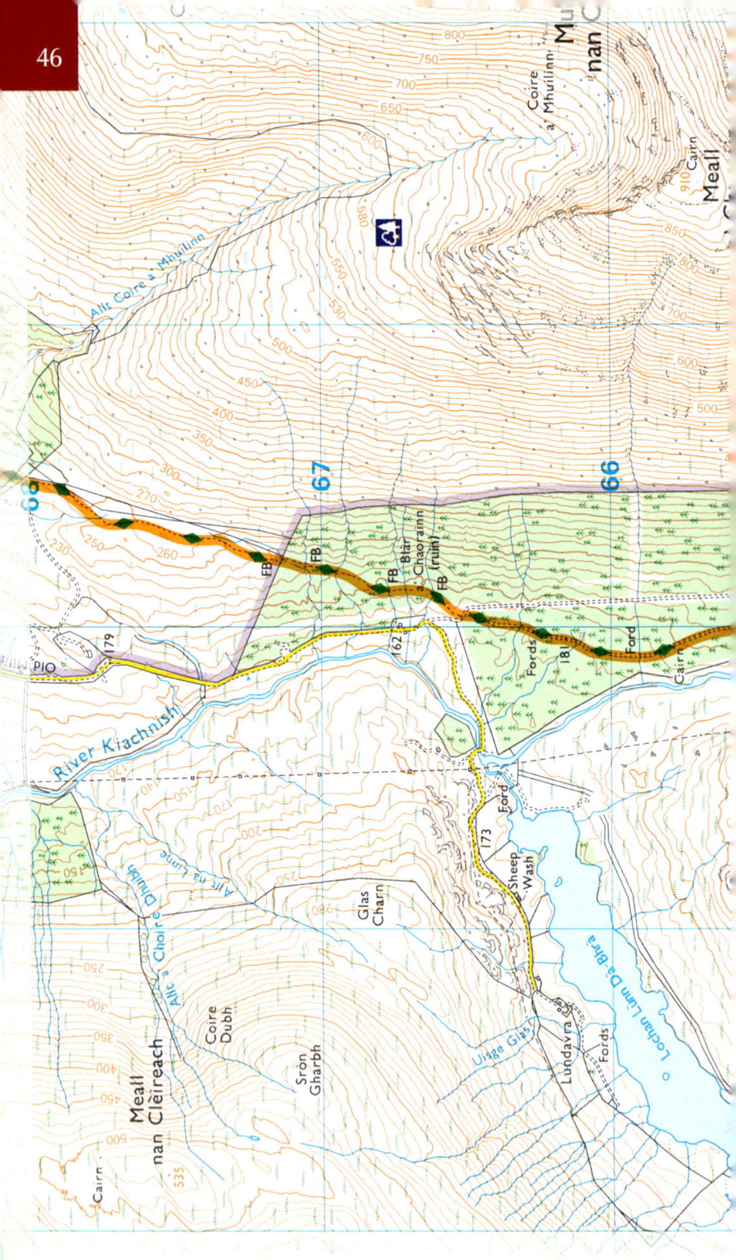
River Kiachnish
Allt Coire a' Mhuilinn
Coire a' Mhuilinn
Meall nan Clèireach
Coire Dubh
Sròn Gharbh
Glas Charn
Allt na Lunne
Allt a' Choire Dhuibh
Blàr a' Chaorainn (ruin)
Sheep Wash
Lundavra
Lochan Lunn Dà-Bhra
Uisge Glas
Ford
Fords
FB
Cairn
Meall
66
67
68

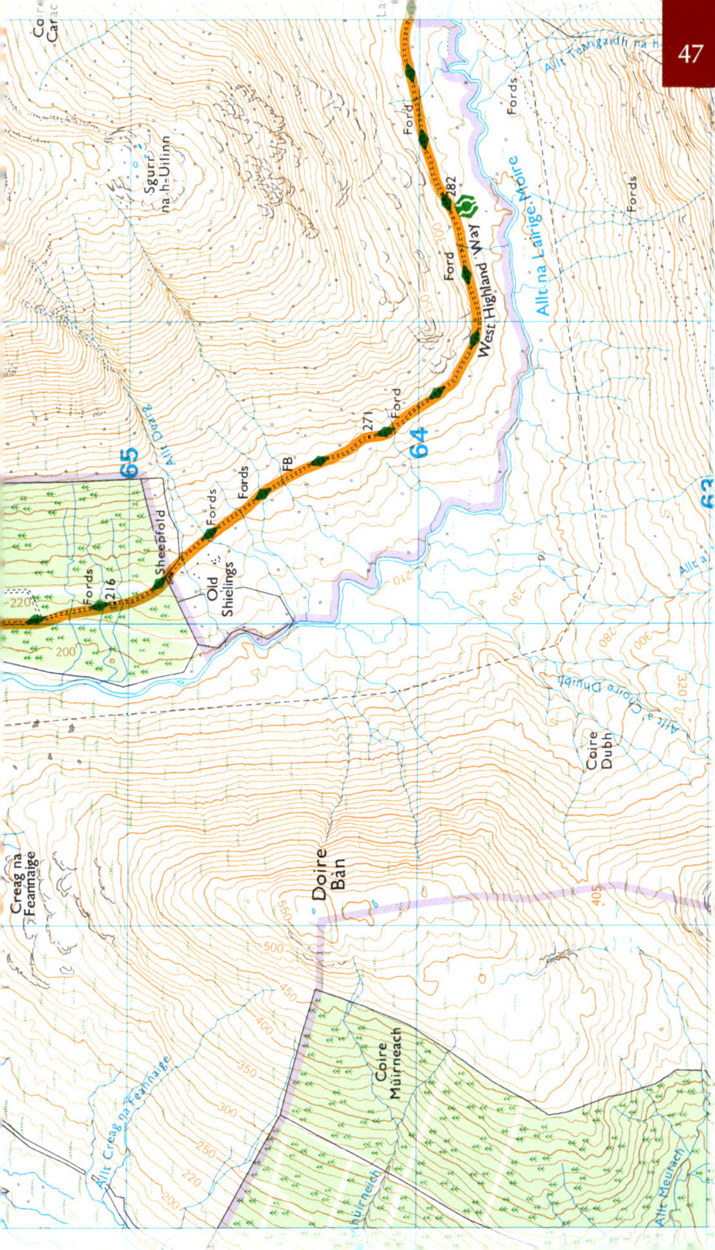
Sgurr na h-Uilinn
Allt Teangaidh na h-
Fords
Ford
282
West Highland Way
Allt na Lairige Mòire
Ford
271
Ford
64
FB
Fords
Fords
65
Allt Dearg
Sheepfold
Old Shielings
Fords
216
220
200
210
230
280
300
320
63
Allt a' Mhe
Allt a' Choire Dhuibh
Coire Dubh
Creag na Feannaige
Doire Bàn
550
500
450
400
350
300
250
220
200
405
Coire Mùirneach
Allt Creag na Feannaige
Mhùirneich
Allt Meurach

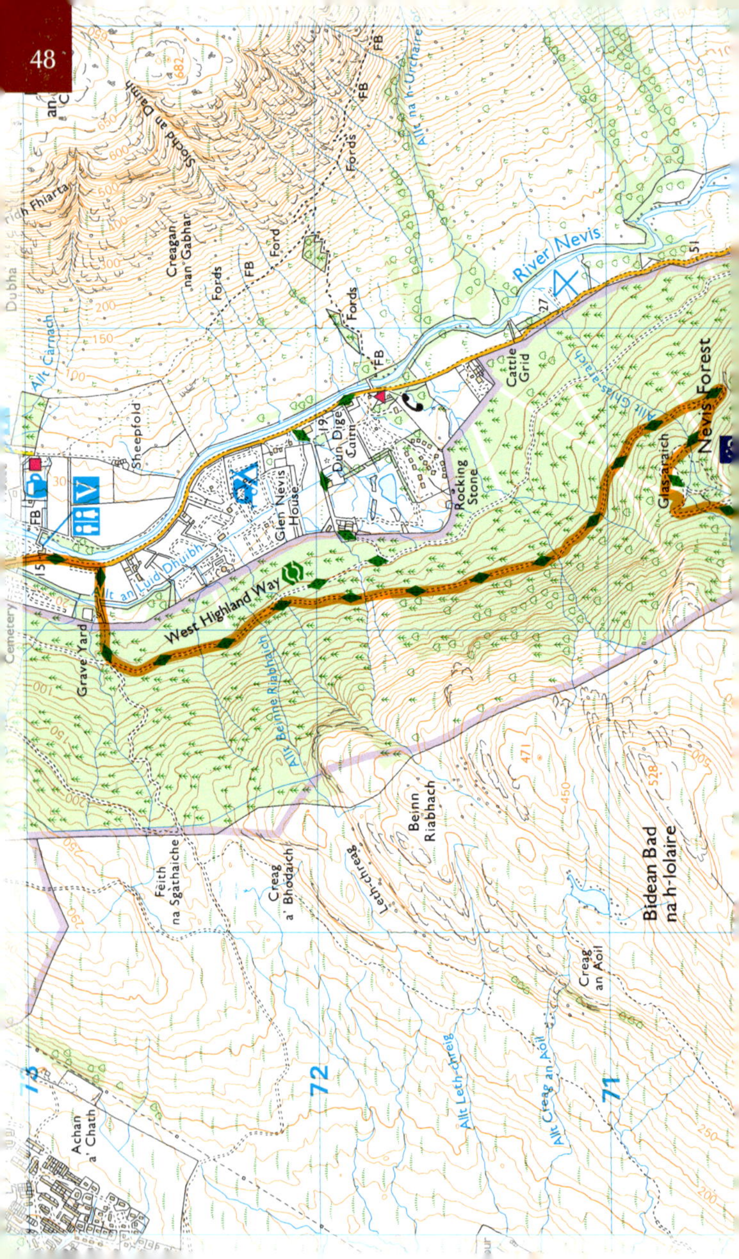

West Highland Way
River Nevis
Glen Nevis House
Dun Dige Cairn
Rocking Stone
Cattle Grid
Nevis Forest
Glas-araich
Allt Ghlas-araich
Grave Yard
Cemetery
Allt an Luid Dhuibh
Allt Beinne Riabhaich
Sheepfold
Allt Carnach
Creagan nan Gabhar
Sloc̀hd an Daimh
Allt na h-Urchaire
Fords
Ford
FB
Beinn Riabhach
Leth-chreag
Creag a' Bhodaich
Feith na Sgàthaiche
Bidean Bad na h-Iolaire
Creag an Aoil
Allt Creag an Aoil
Allt Leth-chreig
Achan a' Chath
Dubha
73
72
71
682
471
528

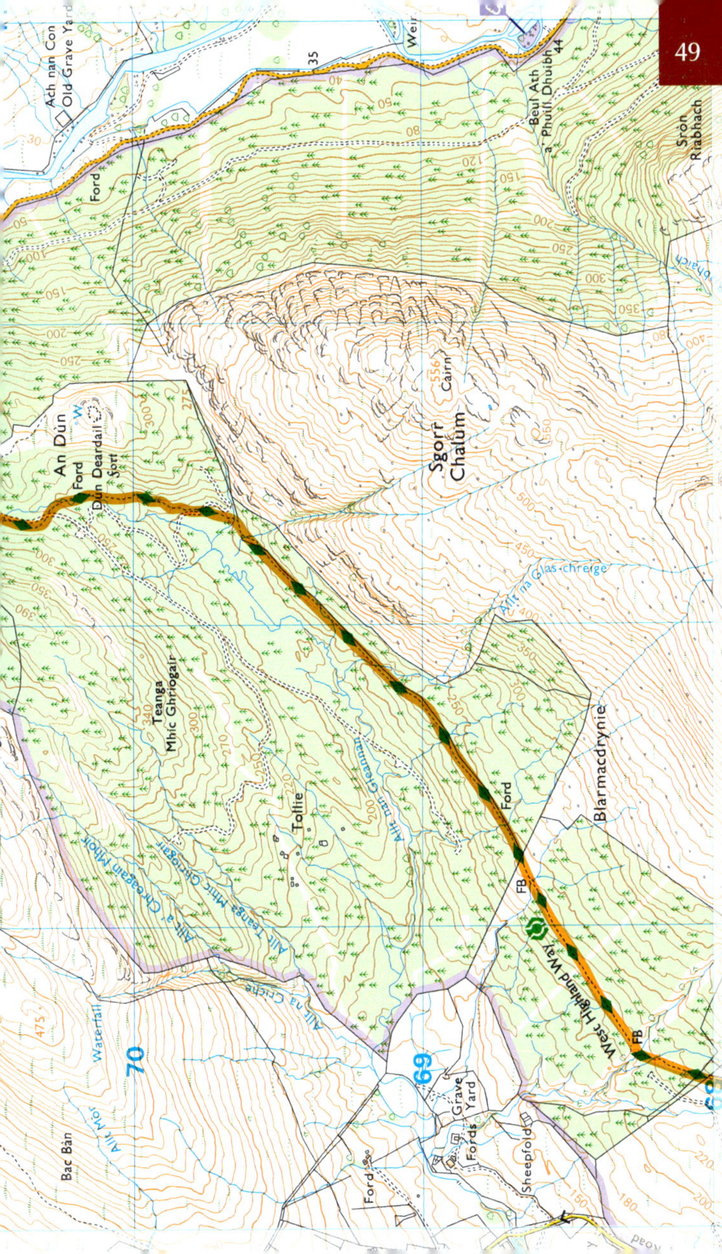
Ach nan Con
Old Grave Yard
Weir
Beul Àth a' Phuill Dhuibh
Sròn Riabhach
Ford
An Dùn
Ford
Dùn Deardail Fort
Sgorr Chalum
Cairn
Allt na Glas-chreige
Teanga Mhic Ghriogair
Tollie
Allt nan Gleannan
Ford
Blarmacdrynie
FB
West Highland Way
FB
Allt Teanga Mhic Ghriogair
Allt a' Chreagain Mhóir
Allt na Criche
Waterfall
Bac Bàn
Allt Mor
Grave Yard
Fords
Sheepfold
Ford

Hall
Rubha Mòr
Ferry P
Underwater Centre
Coll
Fort William
Superstores
Pier
Inverlo
Sch
NTL
Nevis Bridg
FORT WILL
AN GEARA
PO
Hospl
Sch
FB
Piers
Sch
Cow Hill
Fords
Reservoir
Drochaid nan Dathadairean
A 82
Sch
MS
Upper Auchintore
Sch
Achan a' Chath
Cattle Grid
Fèith na Sgàthaiche
An Coireag
Creag a' Bhodaich
Ach' an Todhair
Leth-chreag
Beinn Riabhac
Allt Leth-chreig
Glengour
Clach nan Cairteirean
Allt Creag an Aoil
Creag an Aoil
75
74
73
72
71
78
137
109
288
287
262

Hotel
Works
Shaft
Claggan
Allt Garbh
Creag a' Chàil
479
FB
12
Weirs
Eas a' Chlaiginn
Allt Cas
Creagan Dubh
Sròn Nibheis
Reservoir
Stone
Cam Allt
FBs
Dail an t-Suidhe
FB
Cnocan a' Bhuachaille
Creag an t-Sluichd
Creag Dubh Meall an t-Suidhe
Cemetery
Achintee House
Na Leacan Dubha
An Aisridh Fhiarta
Cairn
Meall an t-Suidhe
711
Cairn
15
FB
Allt Carnach
Grave Yard
Sheepfold
Allt an Luid Dhuibh
Sloched an Daimh
682
Creagan nan Gabhar
West Highland Way
Fords
FB
Ford
Allt Beinne Riabhaich
Glen Nevis House
19
Dun Dige Cairn
Fords
Fords
FB
FB
FB
Allt na h-Urchaire
Rocking Stone
Cattle Grid
471
27
River Nevis

LEGEND OF SYMBOLS USED ON ORDNANCE SURVEY 1:25,000 (EXPLORER) MAPPING

ROADS AND PATHS

Not necessarily rights of way

M1 or A6(M)	Motorway
A 35	Dual carriageway
A30	Main road
B 3074	Secondary road
	Narrow road with passing places
	Road under construction
	Road generally more than 4 m wide
	Road generally less than 4 m wide
	Other road, drive or track, fenced and unfenced
	Gradient: steeper than 20% (1 in 5); 14% (1 in 7) to 20% (1 in 5)
Ferry	Ferry; Ferry P – passenger only
	Path

S Service Area

S Service Area

7 Junction Number

T1 Toll road junction

RAILWAYS

	Multiple track / Single track – standard gauge
	Narrow gauge or Light rapid transit system (LRTS) and station
	Road over; road under; level crossing
	Cutting; tunnel; embankment
	Station, open to passengers; siding

PUBLIC RIGHTS OF WAY

	Footpath
	Bridleway
	Byway open to all traffic
	Restricted byway

The representation on this map of any other road, track or path is no evidence of the existence of a right of way

ARCHAEOLOGICAL AND HISTORICAL INFORMATION

	Site of antiquity
1066	Site of battle (with date)
VILLA	Roman
Castle	Non-Roman
	Visible earthwork

Information provided by English Heritage for England and the Royal Commissions on the Ancient and Historical Monuments for Scotland and Wales

OTHER PUBLIC ACCESS

• • •	Other routes with public access	The exact nature of the rights on these routes and the existence of any restrictions may be checked with the local highway authority. Alignments are based on the best information available
◆ ◆ ◆	Recreational route	
◆ ◆ ◆	National Trail	Long Distance Route
- - - - - -	Permissive footpath	Footpaths and bridleways along which landowners have permitted public use but which are not rights of way. The agreement may be withdrawn
— — —	Permissive bridleway	
• • •	Traffic-free cycle route	
1 1	National cycle network	route number – traffic free; on road

ACCESS LAND

DANGER AREA — Firing and test ranges in the area. Danger! Observe warning notices

MANAGED ACCESS — Access permitted within managed controls, for example, local byelaws. Visit **www.access.mod.uk** for information

Scotland

National Trust for Scotland, always open	
National Trust for Scotland, limited access – observe local signs	
Forestry Commission Land	
Woodland Trust Land	

In Scotland, everyone has access rights in law* over most land and inland water, provided access is exercised responsibly. **This includes walking, cycling, horse-riding and water access, for recreational and educational purposes, and for crossing land or water**. Access rights do not apply to motorised activities, hunting, shooting or fishing, nor if your dog is not under proper control. The **Scottish Outdoor Access Code** is the reference point for responsible behaviour, and can be obtained at **www.outdooraccess-scotland.com** or by phoning your local Scottish Natural Heritage office.

* Land Reform (Scotland) Act 2003

BOUNDARIES

— + — +	National
— · — · —	County (England)
— — — —	Unitary Authority (UA), Metropolitan District (Met Dist), London Borough (LB) or District (Scotland & Wales are solely Unitary Authorities)
· · · · · · ·	Civil Parish (CP) (England) or Community (C) (Wales)
— —	National Park boundary

VEGETATION

Limits of vegetation are defined by positioning of symbols

- Coniferous trees
- Non-coniferous trees
- Coppice
- Orchard
- Scrub
- Bracken, heath or rough grassland
- Marsh, reeds or saltings

HEIGHTS AND NATURAL FEATURES

52 ·	Ground survey height	Surface heights are to the nearest metre above mean sea level. Where two heights are shown, the first height is to the base of the triangulation pillar and the second (in brackets) to the highest natural point of the hill
284 ·	Air survey height	

HEIGHTS AND NATURAL FEATURES (continued)

Vertical face/cliff

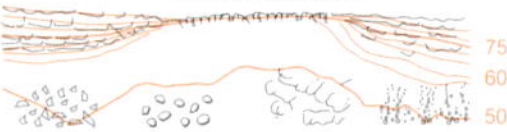

Loose rock

Boulders

Outcrop

Scree

Contours are at 5 or 10 metre vertical intervals

Water

Mud

Sand; sand and shingle

SELECTED TOURIST AND LEISURE INFORMATION

- Building of historic interest
- Cadw
- Heritage centre
- Camp site
- Caravan site
- Camping and caravan site
- Castle / fort
- Cathedral / Abbey
- Craft centre
- Country park
- Cycle trail
- Mountain bike trail
- Cycle hire
- English Heritage
- Fishing
- Forestry Commission Visitor centre
- Garden / arboretum
- Golf course or links
- Historic Scotland
- Information centre, all year
- Information centre, seasonal
- Horse riding
- Museum
- National Park Visitor Centre (park logo) e.g. Yorkshire Dales
- Nature reserve
- National Trust
- Other tourist feature
- Parking
- Park and ride, all year
- Park and ride, seasonal
- Picnic site
- Preserved railway
- PC Public Convenience
- Public house/s
- Recreation / leisure / sports centre
- Roman site (Hadrian's Wall only)
- Slipway
- Telephone, emergency
- Telephone, public
- Telephone, roadside assistance
- Theme / pleasure park
- Viewpoint
- Visitor centre
- Walks / trails
- World Heritage site / area
- Water activites
- Boat trips
- Boat hire

(For complete legend and symbols, see any OS® Explorer map).

THE WEST HIGHLAND WAY

This map booklet accompanies Terry Marsh's guidebook to walking the West Highland Way, described from south to north, between Milngavie on the outskirts of Glasgow and Fort William. The guidebook features annotated 1:100,000 mapping alongside detailed route descriptions plus information on planning your trip and more.

Descending from Tyndrum (Stage 4)